THE OTHER
FALL RIVER TRAGEDY

THE MURDER OF
BERTHA MANCHESTER

THE OTHER FALL RIVER TRAGEDY

THE MURDER OF BERTHA MANCHESTER

by William D. Spencer

NORTH FOREST PRESS

North Forest Press
Knightdale, NC 27545
northforestpress@gmail.com

All rights reserved. *No part of this book may be used or reproduced in any manner whatsoever, scanned, or distributed in any printed or electronic form without written permission from the publisher, except in the case of brief quotations embodied in critical articles and reviews.*

ISBN-13: 9798853796324

Printed in the United States of America on acid-free paper.

Book and cover design by Stefani Koorey, PearTree Press, Westport, MA

Copyright © 2023 by North Forest Press

Printed in the United States of America

Front cover image: Scene on New Boston Road, photographed by George Pitman Brown, May 30, 1893. Courtesy the Fall River Historical Society.

For Tom Spencer

In Memoriam

TABLE OF CONTENTS

List of Illustrations — xi
Introduction — xiii
Source Abbreviations — xv

1. The Manchesters — 1
2. The Breakup — 13
3. The Unthinkable — 17
4. The Investigation Begins — 41
5. The Arrest — 61
6. The Wait — 71
7. The Preliminary Hearing — 81
8. The Wheels of Justice — 87
9. Autumn — 95
10. Finality — 105
11. De Mello vs. Borden — 109
12. Afterward — 129
13. Jose Correa de Mello — 135
14. Afterthoughts — 153

Addendum

1. Reconstructed Preliminary Hearing — 159
2. Grand Jury Indictment of Jose Correiro — 170
3. Plea of Misnomer — 171

Bibliography — 173

LIST OF ILLUSTRATIONS

1.	Stephen Manchester	4
2.	New Boston Road, May 30, 1893	14
3.	Bertha Manchester	17
4.	Bertha Manchester's 8th Grade Test	18
5.	Freddy Manchester	19
6.	Location of the Manchester Farm	24
7.	Manchester House–First Floor	27
8.	Manchester House–Rear View	28
9.	Manchester Kitchen Ell and Well House	29
10.	Manchester Kitchen	30
11.	The Crime Scene	31
12.	Manchester Kitchen Floor Plan	32
13.	Manchester House Floor Plan	33
14.	The Wood Pile	34
15.	Path to Rear of Farm	35
16.	Area Around Manchester House	46
17.	June 2 Police Search	57
18.	Jose Correiro	59
19.	Lacroix Store	62
20.	1879 Trade Dollar	63
21.	Plugged 1879 Half Dollar	63
22.	Wilson Road	64
23.	Prominent Locations	68
24.	Stephen Manchester Testifying at Preliminary Hearing	83
25.	Frank M. Silvia Sr.	140
26.	Joseph M. Chaves Jr.	142
27.	Viscount de Vale da Costa	143
28.	Frank M. Silvia Jr.	145
29.	Frank Wager	146
30.	Dr. Henry A. Rosa	147

INTRODUCTION

In researching *The Case Against Lizzie Borden*, I happened across another Fall River murder, that of Bertha Manchester, who was killed on May 30, 1893. Besides both occurring in the same city, the connection between the cases was that Bertha was murdered just days before Lizzie Borden's trial was to begin and she was killed with an axe, an instrument related to the weapon supposedly responsible for the demise of the Bordens.

A suspect was taken into custody on the evening of the third of June. He was arrested on the fourth and arraigned the morning of Monday, the fifth. Jury selection for the Borden trial began that same morning in New Bedford. The jury was selected by late that afternoon and jurors were immediately sequestered. The Manchester case had been widely publicized, so the twelve men almost certainly knew about it. Probably at least some of them knew an arrest had been made, but even if that were not the case, they knew someone had killed Bertha Manchester a week earlier and that the weapon employed was like that used in the Borden murders. Because Lizzie Borden was in jail, she could not have killed Bertha Manchester; therefore, whoever killed Bertha Manchester might have also killed the Bordens.

Given the proximity in time to Bertha's murder, many thought the Borden jury would be swayed by it, which would bode well for Lizzie Borden. As it turned out, and unbeknownst to them during the time the Borden jury was sequestered, it became apparent that the two cases were not related. However, the Manchester case deserves further consideration, which, heretofore, as far as I can tell, it has not had. Almost everyone knows about the deaths of Andrew and Abby Borden, but almost no one remembers the brutal death of Bertha Manchester. It is time for her story to be told.

In *The Case Against Lizzie Borden*, I devoted considerable time to the ethos of late-nineteenth-century New England and how it might have affected the case. Even though the very same ethos applied to the Manchester murder, how it played out was in stark contrast to in the Borden crimes.

In the Borden book, I strove to use public records to describe the events surrounding the Borden murders, which abound due to the notoriety of the case. The inquest, preliminary hearing, and trial testimonies have all been preserved. The record books of most of the police officers involved on the case are also available. I avoided, to the greatest extent possible, newspaper accounts. The three major Fall River newspapers fought for readership and seemed to have no difficulty in reporting whatever rumors or unsubstantiated stories that the reporters came across.

Unfortunately, to my knowledge, not one such document exists in the Manchester case. Unlike the Borden case, no inquest was held. There was a one-day preliminary hearing, the record of which has been lost. Fortunately, the *Fall River Daily Herald* reprinted what appears to be at least most of the complete testimony of Bertha's father, Stephen Manchester. The case did not go to trial.

Given these circumstances, one must rely on the newspapers to fill in many of the blanks. It should be noted that, in the first few days after the murders, the Manchester case got every bit as much press coverage as had the Borden murders during the same span—even some of the same journalists covered both cases. By all appearances, the Manchester murder was covered professionally, at least according to the standards of the time. Yet, besides the fact that the Manchester case was effectively solved within a few days, the difference between these gruesome acts is that Bertha Manchester was a farm girl and the culprit, even before his identification, was supposed to be one of "the usual suspects." Thus, there was no sensational aspect of the case on which the newspapers could feed other than the short-lived possibility that a mass murderer was still on the loose.

But that is the central point here. Why does society somehow equate fame or, in the case of the Bordens, gender and wealth, with how we report and cover a murder? Should the Bordens be remembered and Bertha Manchester, killed even more brutally, be forgotten? This book seeks to explore these issues.

SOURCE ABBREVIATIONS

BG–*Boston Globe*

FRDEN–*Fall River Daily Evening News*

FRDH–*Fall River Daily Herald*

FRDG–*Fall River Daily Globe*

PL–*Parallel Lives: A Social History of Lizzie A. Borden and Her Fall River*. Michael Martins and Dennis Binette. Fall River: Fall River Historical Society, 2011.

CHAPTER 1
THE MANCHESTERS

The best-known family name in the history of Fall River, Massachusetts, is that of the Bordens, due to the well-publicized murders of Andrew and Abby Borden in 1892. The first Borden to come to America was Richard, in 1635. Some of his descendants became amongst the wealthiest patrons of nineteenth-century Fall River, but Andrew was not one of those select few.

Family lore is that Thomas Manchester came to the New World in the late 1600s, meaning that the Manchesters date almost as far back in the colonies as did the Bordens. None of them, however, became prominent in Fall River.

On March 28, 1761, John Manchester was born in Tiverton, Rhode Island. Tiverton and Fall River are adjacent, with the Massachusetts-Rhode Island state line dividing the two. However, at the time of John's birth, the state boundary was in dispute. In 1862, this was settled, with the southern part of Tiverton becoming Rhode Island and the northern part becoming annexed into Fall River. Thus, it is possible that John was born in an area that later became part of Fall River. In any event, the Manchesters were clearly in the Fall River area by that point. On April 24, 1785, John married Mary Brayton, also of Tiverton. Some of the Fall River Braytons, it might be noted, *did* acquire great wealth. On August 17, 1787, the couple had a son, Benjamin.

In his mid-twenties, Benjamin joined the army and fought in the War of 1812. Around this time, he married Lucannah Cook. The couple had thirteen children, reported to have been: Abram, Silas, Frank, Andrew, Rhoda, Delaney, Alexander, Nancy, Mary, Stephen, Lucannah (Lucy), James, and Almira.

According to the *Fall River Daily Herald*:

> Frank was drowned when a young man near the old ferry slip and Andrew, who was a sea faring man, was lost overboard on a whaling voyage. (*FRDH*, May 31, 1893)

Given the time period in question and the fact that the Manchesters were a typical working family, it is not unusual that nothing of note can be found about them through the first half of the nineteenth century. The 1850 U.S. census shows that Benjamin was a farmer in Tiverton. By 1860, his residence was shown as Fall River, but he is now listed as "infirm."

At some point (or points), Benjamin eventually acquired several properties on South Main Street, near Spring Street, in downtown Fall River.

Benjamin's son Stephen was born on July 28, 1829. (Stephen claimed he was born in 1830, but contemporary records tend to substantiate the earlier date.) He is shown as still being with the family in the 1850 census but, at twenty-one, is shown to be a sailor, hardly an occupation one would have on a farm. The term "sailor" may conjure images of someone in the navy, or possibly involved in transatlantic shipping. However, Stephen was a sailor in a much broader sense—like his uncle Andrew before him, he worked in the whaling industry.

In the mid-1800s, most of the options for working class men did not require a great deal of skill. They did, however, often involve danger. Stable keepers, for example, could be kicked by horses, sometimes with fatal results. But most of such jobs in Fall River were in the mills. Many a finger was lost in the machines. Far worse, the close, humid environment in the mills was a breeding ground for tuberculosis and other communicable diseases.

Life aboard a whaling ship is thusly described:

> The forecastle was black and slimy with filth, very small and hot as an oven. It was filled with a compound of foul air, smoke, sea-chests, soap-kegs, greasy pans, tainted meat, sea-sick Americans and foreign ruffians. The ruffians were smoking, laughing, chattering and cursing the green hands who were sick. With groans on one side, and yells, oaths, laughter and smoke on the other, it altogether did not impress [me] as a very pleasant home for the next year or two. [I was] indeed, sick and sorry enough, and heartily wished [myself] ashore.

Etchings of a Whaling Cruise, J. Ross Browne, 1846 (24)

One might posit that Stephen's choice of leaving the city to work at sea seemed perhaps no better or worse than his land-based alternatives. But, in fact, there was an aspect of whaling that made it less appealing than staying in Fall River. The mill worker, blacksmith, or salesman could go to his home and family each night, and typically have at least Sundays off. But once the whaler left port, he would not see any family member for some time.

> The larger a vessel, the greater distances it could travel. The whaling schooner, the smallest whaler, generally undertook

6-month voyages, while brigs, barks, and ships might be at sea for three or four years. The longest whaling voyage is believed to be that of the Ship *Nile* from 1858 to 1869 — eleven years!

New Bedford Whaling Museum

Despite this dismal outlook, on October 26, 1849, at age twenty, Stephen Cook Manchester received his certificate of protection and became a whaler. (Certificates of protection dated back to 1796 when the British began impressing foreign seamen, and these certificates continued through the mid 1800s.)

Another difference between land-based jobs and whaling was the method of payment. Laborers typically were paid each day if they were doing random jobs, or by the week if employed in an ongoing position. Thus at least the worker usually had a good idea of what his daily or weekly income would be. Whalers were quite a different story.

As Ishmael said in *Moby Dick*:

> I was already aware that in the whaling business they paid no wages; but all hands, including the captain received certain shares of the profits called lays, and that these lays were proportional to the degree of importance pertaining to the respective duties of the ship's company. (*Moby Dick*, 91)

There was no way to know how successful, or how long, each voyage would be. The sailor signed on knowing his percentage but had no way to know what the end profit would be. Good voyages could result in quite a payoff, but in theory a sailor could invest two years at sea and have little or nothing to show for it in the end.

Upon signing his certificate, Stephen became a crewman on the *Caravan*, which sailed from Fall River. He is listed as light complexioned. Even for the mid 1800s, Stephen was a small man, being only 5'4¾" tall. It would be supposed that before signing up for a whaling expedition that one would investigate what to expect. He would probably be told something like what J. Ross Browne said above. And he would know that he would be at sea for some time and get a percentage of some currently unknown profit. But there is a difference between hearing a description and the actual experience of two years at sea. Given that, it would be deduced that many did not sign up for a second "cruise." Stephen Manchester, however, liked what he saw, or at least did not seem to see any better career alternative. In 1852, Stephen signed up on the *Polar Star*. (This and future voyages sailed from New Bedford.) He was now a "boat steerer," meaning he steered the small boats sent by the ship to kill the whales. Records show that the ship left port for the Pacific on October 11, 1852. Of course, at this time in history, to go from New Bedford to the Pacific meant the ship had to sail around South America, hence at least one reason for the extended expedition times. The *Polar Star* did not return until June 11, 1856. As a boat steerer, Stephen was due 1/80 of the voyage's profits, although we do not know what those were. By comparison, a "greenhand" got 1/200; a seaman, 1/175; the first mate; 1/20. Records indicate that the first mate on the *Polar Star* was named Thomas Manchester. He had begun whaling in 1828 at the age of seventeen. Since the men were probably relatives, this may be how Stephen first became interested in whaling.

1. Stephen Manchester (Courtesy Stephen M. Hart).

Stephen was again on the *Polar Star* when it left port on August 26, 1856. (Thus, after more than three-and-a-half years at sea, Stephen was on land only two months before his next multi-year voyage.) We may see here why Stephen kept at whaling. He probably made around 1/200 of the profit on his first voyage. On his second, he made 1/80. When the *Polar Star* left New Bedford in August, Stephen was the second mate, earning 1/40 of the profits.

Whaling records indicate that, in 1862, he transferred to the bark *Tamerlane* as the first mate, with a profit fraction of probably about 1/20. His complexion was now listed as dark, undoubtedly due to more than ten years at sea. At this point, the Civil War was raging. His draft registration record, dated June 1863, indicates he was "on a whaling voyage." As such, he avoided service in the Civil War.

When the *Tamerlane* returned to port in 1865, records show Stephen signed up for yet another voyage, this time on the *Seine*. For some reason, his skin was now again light. Records indicate that the *Seine* left for the Pacific on November 1, 1865, and did not return to port until 1870.

However, Fall River records contradict these movements. There is no question that, on September 11, 1864, he married Hannah M. Davis in Fall River. It should be noted that the attending clergyman was listed as Charles A. Snow. Indeed, Snow was the pastor of the Third Street Baptist Church at the time, so it was not as if the couple was somehow married elsewhere, and the marriage only recorded in Fall River. Moreover, the couple was hardly married on a whaling vessel in the Pacific Ocean. However, it is noted that on the marriage record Stephen's occupation is listed as still a "mariner." He and his wife Hannah are shown living with his sister Mary in Fall River in the 1865 Massachusetts census. At the 1893 divorce hearing, Manchester said he had owned the same farm in Fall River for twenty-six years. He, therefore, first occupied the farm in about 1867. The 1869 Fall River city directory verifies that Stephen C. Manchester was a farmer on New Boston Road. He had a son born in Fall River in 1866, and a daughter in 1868.

There are so many independent documents for the period of 1864 to 1870 that the whaling records had to be in error to some extent. Stephen could not be on a ship that was at sea from 1862 until 1865, and on another ship that sailed from 1865 until 1870, even though the descriptions of Stephen on the two ships' records match exactly with his name, age, and residence of Fall River.

In the case of the *Tamerlane*, three possibilities seem to stand out. One is that he sailed on a different ship that returned to the U.S. sometime before September of 1864. Another is that, like Herman Melville, he abandoned ship at some intermediate port and returned to Fall River, although, in that event, he would not have been paid for his time on the ship. The third is that he did not sail on any ship whatsoever. This possibility emerges from the records of the *Seine*. Here, too, the description of Stephen was correct, yet it is impossible that he was on that or any other ship. Could it be that in 1862, most likely to avoid being drafted into the army, he paid someone to sail on the *Tamerlane* under his name? When that ship returned, the man decided to sail on the *Seine*. However, by then, he was known as Stephen Manchester, and thus signed up under that name.

The above are merely examples of what might have happened. Others are limited, whether benign or otherwise, only by the limits of one's imagination. Overall, however, we must consider the above as anomalies of history. They do not alter the overall picture: Stephen Manchester was a sailor from 1849 until at least the early-1860s. He first married in 1864, by which time he was already thirty-five years old. (His wife was only twenty-two, however.) By the late 1860s, he had bought a farm, and he continued in that occupation, at that location, until his death.

Not long after her marriage, Hannah had the couple's first child, Harry E., on March 3, 1866. (Stephen's occupation is still shown as "mariner.") Daughter Jennie followed on December 10, 1868. Stephen is now listed as a farmer. The second daughter, Bertha M., was born on May 7, 1871, and son Frederick (known as Freddie) on December 10, 1881. We thus see the unusual coincidence that of the couple's four children, two shared the same birthday.

Stephen's farm grew over the years. In 1870, shortly after acquiring it, it comprised thirteen improved acres and thirteen additional unimproved acres. He had seven milking cows, one other cattle, and two horses. He grew corn, oats, barley, potatoes, hay, and harvested forest products. He estimated the farm to be worth $1,800 and its machinery another $250. The livestock was worth $430 and farm production totaled $1,270.

By 1880, he claimed twenty-five acres of tilled land, plus ten of meadow. He estimated the farm to be worth $12,000, plus $300 in machinery and $1,200 in livestock. He now had seventeen milk cows and estimated they had produced more than 12,000 gallons of milk the previous year. By 1893, Stephen had twenty milk cows. Overall, it appears he was doing well.

Bridget Sullivan was the servant for the Borden family. The Bordens were, of course, wealthy, but as was pointed out in *The Case Against Lizzie Borden*, the term servant was somewhat ambiguous. A servant in one household might not have the same duties as a servant in another. It was not unusual for young women to act as servants in even more modest households. In the 1880 census, Mary Benny, age twenty-two, is listed as being a servant in the Manchester household.

Sadly, Hannah Manchester died at the age of thirty-nine on January 17, 1882, of bronchitis. Her youngest child, Freddie, was just one month old. At first, Stephen's sister Lucy, and then daughter Jennie, acted as the housekeeper, although it is not clear how newborn Freddie was cared for, since he would have needed breast milk.

In the early 1860s, Samuel Whittles Jr., of Oldham, Lancashire, England, married a woman named Mary, or possibly Mary Ann. On June 14, 1864, Mary gave birth to a son, James Dutton Whittles.

By 1871, Mary apparently had died, and Samuel Jr., along with son James, were living with Samuel's parents in Oldham. Also now in the family unit was Samuel Jr.'s sister, Mary Jane.

The England census of that year shows twenty-eight-year-old Samuel Jr. to be an unemployed grocer. Perhaps because of his employment situation, or rather the lack of it, Samuel sailed for the United States, but left son James in the care of his parents. Samuel settled in Fall River in 1872 or 1873. He got work as a laborer, but soon secured employment, not surprisingly, at the grocer Cobb, Bates and Yerxa at 99 South Main Street. By coincidence, this was almost across the street from the 92 South Main Street building Andrew Borden owned at the time of his murder in 1892. In 1876, Samuel Jr. married Mary A. Nuttall. In nineteenth-century Fall River, the coincidences seem endless. The couple occupied the house at 11 Ferry Street a house once owned by Andrew Borden's father and later by Andrew. It had, in turn, been purchased by Henry Nuttall, the father of Stephen's wife. Nuttall had lived in the house, but in 1875 moved to 36 Stafford Road. Samuel's son James came to Fall River about the time of the marriage, but he is not listed as being a member of Samuel's household in the 1880 census, even though James would have been fifteen or sixteen at that time. In fact, James is not evident in the census for some reason.

There is no doubt that Samuel Jr. was in the United States for good, as in 1880 he became a U.S. citizen. By 1882, the couple had moved almost across the street, to 8 Ferry. Eventually, they had three sons.

The 1881 England census shows sixty-four-year-old father Samuel Sr., sixty-one-year-old wife Emma, and their thirty-nine-year-old unmarried daughter, Mary Jane, now residing in Rochdale, a few miles north of Oldham. When the Borden daughters reached their majority, father Andrew afforded them the lives of unmarried upper-class women. They received a yearly stipend from Andrew and never worked a day in their lives. Clearly mill-worker Samuel Sr. could provide no such accommodations, even if he had so wanted. Mary Jane worked in the Lancashire mills since at least the age of seventeen.

For whatever reason, in 1882 or 1883, the elder Whittles, along with daughter Mary Jane, decided to emigrate to Fall River. The 1884 Fall River city directory shows all the Whittles, except James, living at 8 Ferry Street. In an era before social security networks, the elder Samuel Whittles still needed to work and obtained employment in one of the Fall River mills. On Christmas Day, 1888, James married Minnie Bence of Fall River. Those familiar with the Borden murder case will recognize the surname. Minnie's brother Eli was the pharmacist at Smith's drug store when a woman purported to be Lizzie Borden came in and attempted to purchase prussic acid.

A woman with twenty years' experience in the Lancashire mills would have had no trouble in obtaining employment in one of the similar Fall River mills. However, it does not appear that daughter Mary Jane went to work in one. If she did, it was short lived. Since her mother's death, Jennie Manchester had acted as that family's housekeeper. However, Mary Jane Whittles soon accepted that position.

Life was difficult in the late nineteenth century. Traditionally, the man worked and the woman kept the house and raised the children. Today, a parent might be able to do both, but this was next to impossible in the 1890s. There were no labor-saving devices, no social life nets. As a result, those who lost a partner often remarried much more quickly than a normal mourning period and the development of romantic interest might take today. Perhaps because of this, on May 28, 1884, Stephen Manchester married Mary Jane Whittles. This was her first marriage but, at forty-one, much like Abby Gray, the suitors had most certainly stopped calling. Under these circumstances described above, it would be deduced that many second marriages were those of convenience. As we shall see, this marriage has the appearance of being one of these.

Stephen's daughter Jennie married William W. Coolidge of Fall River on April 30, 1889. Coolidge ran a men's clothing store at 84 Pleasant Street. The couple lived at 49 Quarry Street.

On paper, things looked reasonably bright for the Manchesters, the Nuttalls, and the Whittles. The Manchesters seem to have recovered as best they could after the death of Hannah. The Nuttalls had seen their daughter marry an up-and-coming citizen. Arguably, the Whittles lot seemed the brightest. In 1870, Samuel and Emma Whittles may have been satisfied with their lot, but son Samuel Jr. was unemployed and daughter Mary Jane looked as though she was destined for a life in the mills of Lancashire. Now, fifteen years later, the entire family was living in a new country. Samuel Sr. again got mill work. Son Samuel Jr. was gainfully employed, well respected in the community, married, and had three children. Daughter Mary Jane had found a husband and, in 1885, she bore a son, Alexander.

But life does not play out on paper. It certainly did so on the farms, roads, and ponds of Fall River.

On June 9, 1887, Stephen was working on his farm, removing rocks from one of his fields. The stone was a large one, and two oxen were employed to move it. A chain was wound around the rock and fastened to the beasts. A friend, thirty-five-year-old Patrick Kiely of Fountain Street, went behind the rock and put a lever underneath it to help in the excavation. The oxen were prodded forward and managed to move the rock somewhat, but then the chain snapped. Kiely was still standing behind the rock, which now fell back into its original position. This caused the lever Kiely was holding to snap back violently, striking him in the head and killing him instantly. The death was written off as a farm accident, which indeed it was, but it was certainly a day Stephen Manchester would never forget.

In 1892, Edward Dwelley stole money from Stephen Manchester. On August 12 of that year, Dwelley pleaded guilty of the theft and was sentenced to the Massachusetts Reformatory.

As was mentioned, Henry Nuttall, the father-in-law of Stephen Whittles Jr., moved from Ferry Street to Stafford Road. On June 20, 1887, only eleven days after the Manchester farm accident, Nuttall harnessed a horse to a two-wheeled dog cart and left his house, in the company of a Mr. Sutcliffe. It was the first time the horse had ever been hitched to this cart, and the strange vehicle soon spooked him. The horse reared and took off. Sutcliffe was unscathed, but Nuttall was thrown violently to the ground. He died within an hour. (Two months later, with a new owner, the horse broke away on Pleasant Street and collided with several teams. This time, however, there were no injuries.)

The worst was yet to come.

Sunday, May 25, 1890, was a pleasant spring day. A group of twelve, including the entire Samuel Whittles Jr. family, gathered to spend the day in the woods on the banks of Watuppa Pond. They attempted to secure a boat to cross the pond but were unable to do so. Therefore, the group made the long walk around the pond to its other side. Samuel was a member of the Humboldt Club, a scientific organization. The club had a camera that it lent to its members on a rotating basis. Today it was Samuel's turn, and he enthusiastically took pictures of the scenery he encountered. There was a small island in the center of the pond, and Samuel felt it would be a good destination for photographs. However, the group had no way to reach it. As chance would have it, a man named Fred Parkinson happened to be nearby, and he had a boat with him. A deal was made, and the party obtained the use of the boat until two o'clock.

In all, this would seem like just another event on just another spring day. But there were problems. The first is that the boat could safely hold perhaps eight people, but the party comprised twelve, all of whom boarded the craft. The boat was also more like a raft, having a flat bottom and thus unstable. The group could not procure a sail, so the slightly built Walter Turner was chosen to row the craft. The slow progress that resulted from the efforts of the lone rower meant that the craft was to take quite some time to reach the island. During this time, the winds picked up. First, the water became choppy, but eventually this turned to whitecaps.

Given the circumstances, the party decided to abandon the quest for the island and to head for shore near the water pumping station. However, the strong winds soon drove the unstable craft off course and toward a rocky area of the coastline. As the boat approached the rocks, the spraying water entered the craft. The wind, choppy water, and water taken on combined to make the boat rock and even more water came into it. With a final lurch, the boat capsized, throwing all into the churning water.

A fireman at the pumping station witnessed the event and rushed to the area. However, his going was slow because of a heavy thicket. By the time he reached the shore near where the boat had capsized, he saw four people. Eight had sunk out of sight.

Walter Turner somehow had been able to swim to shore. Another of the group, John Buckley, also made shore. George Hamer clung to the gunwales of the overturned boat. When ten-year-old Edwin Whittles came to the surface, Hamer grabbed him and pulled him to the gunwales. The craft, now unencumbered, drifted toward the shore and the two were rescued. (It might be noted that Edwin lived until the age of ninety-five.)

Many had heard the calls from the boat and had headed, via boat and land, to the site. Eventually, eight bodies were recovered and laid on the beach.

In the late-nineteenth century, the factories, mines, diseases, and even daily life saw to it that life was hard – and cheap. So, too, was it for the Manchesters, the Nuttalls, and the Whittles.

Stephen Manchester spent all his early years as a whaler. There were no newspaper reporters on whaling ships and even if there had been they would have had no way to publish their stories, at least as they unfolded. One reading books such as *Moby Dick* sees how miserable this life was, not to mention dangerous. Upon leaving this profession, Stephen bought a farm – a normal enough thing to do in those times. He married and had children. But his still-young wife died just after giving birth, leaving him with four children to raise alone while trying single-handedly to run a dairy farm and deliver milk every day. Three years after remarrying, Stephen witnessed one man die on his farm. Five years later, a man stole sufficient money from Stephen Manchester to be sent to prison.

By the standards of the time, the Nuttalls appeared to have gone through life relatively unscathed. Yet, in the blink of an eye, patriarch Henry died in a violent accident.

The Whittalls had lived an apparently hard life in England and looked to improve their lot in the burgeoning United States. Step by step, the family did so. Yet, in an instant, they lost a son and two grandchildren. In the accident, the Nuttalls lost those same grandchildren and a daughter.

Each of the tragedies enumerated here was worthy of an article in the local newspapers. But soon the newspapers would be covering an event comparable to the Borden murders. Like those murders, this event merited months of coverage. And the Manchester family would never be the same again.

CHAPTER 2
THE BREAKUP

Mary Ann Whittles married Stephen Manchester in 1884 and had a son soon afterwards. In the next five years, she had to endure the loss of all but one of her brother's family. But, unfortunately, her domestic situation did not provide any offsetting comfort. The marriage quickly began to fall apart.

On January 6, 1888, Mary Ann entered a petition of separate support from her husband. For some reason, the suit was dismissed.

Things did not improve from this point forward. On December 8, 1892, Stephen filed a libel suit for divorce, stating he had:

> Always been faithful to his marriage vows and obligations, but the said Mary J. Manchester, being wholly regardless of the same, at said Fall River in the month of July, A.D. 1888, utterly deserted him and has continued such desertion from that time to the date hereof. (From divorce filing; *PL*, 496 - 497)

Mary Jane Manchester was not the type of woman who was satisfied with being on the defensive. Therefore, in response to Stephen's petition, on January 17, 1893, her attorney, Milton Reed, made a motion for alimony during the pendency of the case. Stephen's attorney, A. E. Bragg, opposed the motion, and the case was continued until the next day.

The three daily Fall River newspapers routinely reported on the activities of the Superior Court and were thus present for the various cases to be presented on January 18 before Judge Caleb Blodgett. (In six months, Blodgett would be one of the justices at the Borden trial.) These were typically of a perfunctory nature. However, the *Fall River Daily News* reported:

> The superior court adjourned for the term at five minutes before 4 yesterday. The afternoon's business was less varied than that of the forenoon, but embodied more interesting features. The first case disposed of was marked by peculiarly dramatic and memorial incidents. The case was that of Mary J. Manchester,

wife of Stephen C. Manchester, the New Boston Road farmer, who on the 8th of last December filed a libel in this court seeking a divorce from his wife on the ground of desertion. The petitioner in yesterday's case sought alimony, being unable to support herself. (Jan. 19, 1893)

2. Scene on New Boston Road, photographed by George Pitman Brown, May 30, 1893. Courtesy the Fall River Historical Society.

According to the *Fall River Daily Globe*, Stephen took the stand and testified that:

> ... his wife had deserted him three times and the last time she remained away about three years. One day she came to his house on New Boston road, and he told her to get out and stay out. (*FRDG*, Jan. 19, 1893)

According to Stephen, the trouble between the couple was due to their child, Alexander. As a dairy farmer, Stephen said what limited sleep he got was important but that Mary Jane "let" the child cry all night. According to him, on one occasion, the following conversation occurred:

> Mr. Manchester - "Is there no way to stop that kid from yelling?"
>
> Wife - "No, not that I know of."

Husband - "Yes there is."

Wife - "How?"

Husband - "Spank it. And if you don't, I will throw it out the window."

(*FRDG*, Jan. 19, 1893)

Stephen did not follow through with his threat, but, needless to say, his wife was not amused with the proposed solution.

A second serious incident occurred a year or so later. Asked if he had ever horsewhipped the boy, Stephen told the following story:

> No, but I struck him with a stick, and I will tell you how it happened. I had a Bramah [actually, "Brama"] rooster which cost $6, and it was sick. I put it under the barn, and one day I caught that young shaver pounding it with a stick. He was laying it onto that rooster in good shape, and I just got at him. And as I did, the old woman came out of the house. Now, judge, I caught whales in the Indian ocean, and I have seen the sea roll, heard the thunder peal, saw the lightning flash, but the combined fury of the elements never was in it with that wife of mine. She came out with her foresail, her spanker broom and her spinnaker set with the wind blowing a gale from her rear, and I never saw anything like it. (*FRDG*, Jan. 19, 1893)

Reed, the attorney for Mary Jane, asked Stephen how old the boy was. His response was, "old enough to throw stones at me." (Later testimony indicated Alexander was about eighteen months old at the time.)

Stephen's conduct as a witness was not common in the Superior Court. The *News* described it thusly:

> Mr. Manchester testified in the most vivid manner, alike as to speech and gestures. Having once been a sailor, he mixed the idiom of the sea with his landlubber phrases in a way that at once won the ears and started the risibles of all present. He was candid, evidently, in at least some of his statements, and as for the others, he showed he had been, in his own estimation, the Great Henpecked Husband of the Age. His description of the crucial combat in his domestic infelicities was extremely graphic. He was not, like most witnesses, cabined, cribbed and confined to the witness stand [at that time, witnesses stood while testifying], but he let himself out in an extraordinary manner, for several minutes departing so far from the conventional as to step from the stand, and with full play of facial muscles, exercise of arms, bow of the legs and use of lung power, describe his sufferings as a married man. (*FRDEN*, Jan. 19, 1893)

The *Fall River Daily Herald* added:

> [Manchester said] he did not want his wife and could not live with her, as she had done everything possible to aggravate him.

> When he was in a passion he was the coolest man in the world. The remarks of Mr. Manchester caused a great deal of amusement in the court room, and his dramatic gestures were worthy of a better cause. (Jan. 19, 1893)

Mary Jane was then called to the stand and, given the lack of description by the newspapers, appears to have been a more conventional witness. According to her, Stephen "kicked her and once he pulled a chair away as she attempted to be seated, and she fell upon the floor." (In his testimony, Stephen had denied ever hitting her.)

The court adjourned with no follow-up date set, apparently because it was the final session of the term. During the hearing, according to the *News*, "Dr. Dwight E. Cone testified that Mary Jane's bodily condition was such as to prevent her earning a living, and she herself testified to that effect." Thus, before adjourning, Blodgett granted Mary Jane $30, to be payable within ten days, and $3 per week during the pending of the suit. Stephen paid the $30 on January 28 (*PL*, 497).

On January 20, having just heard her husband's testimony on the matter, Mary Jane decided to enter her own suit for divorce, based on the grounds of cruel and abusive treatment. Like her husband, she sought custody of Alexander.

It would be many months before the Manchester divorce was again addressed in the courtroom.

CHAPTER 3
THE UNTHINKABLE

With the divorce suits in limbo at the will of the courts, life returned to normal for Stephen Manchester; that is, life without Mary Jane and Alexander had been the norm for several years. The family unit on the New Boston Road farm consisted only of Stephen, daughter Bertha, and son Freddie. Bertha was now twenty-two and has assumed responsibility for running the house. From time-to-time, Stephen hired a woman to help Bertha, but none was so employed at this time.

3. Bertha Manchester. From the *Fall River Daily Herald*, May 31, 1893.

In the Borden family, running the house meant just that. But Bertha lived on a farm. Even more to the point, the family's main source of income was the dairy herd of twenty cows. Crops in the field do not necessarily need daily maintenance, but animals do. Bertha fed all the animals and even operated the mowing machine. Her daily work had hardly begun once the cooking and laundry was finished. By all accounts, she was a strong girl and a hard worker. If she was dissatisfied with her lot in life, she apparently did not express it.

4. Bertha Manchester's School Test (Courtesy Stephen M. Hart).

The above paints a picture of Bertha as a simple farm girl. But clearly, she had had her dreams. One could think, given his background, Stephen

Manchester might disdain formal education, especially for his daughters. But Jennie had graduated from high school and, by all indications, Bertha also would have done so had it not been for the rift existing between Stephen and Mary Jane.

Somehow preserved is a school test of Bertha's. We note that not only is her penmanship superb, so is her writing. It would appear this test dates from a time when she was in her early teens. This corresponds to the period when her father married for the second time. Yet despite the turmoil in the Manchester house and the supposition that Bertha had many farm duties by that age, she was able to apply herself to her lessons, attested to by her grade of 99 on her test. (It appears her teacher overlooked Bertha's consistent misspelling of "participle.")

Freddie was now twelve and helped on the farm. Often, he would accompany his father on the milk delivery route into the heart of the city, four miles south of the farm. Stephen, of course, had to be up hours before that, milking the cows.

5. Freddie Manchester. From the *Fall River Daily Globe*, June 1, 1893.

In looking at old census records, it is common to see large farm families. As each child aged, he or she was assigned more work. Teenage children were expected to act as de facto farm hands. By comparison, Stephen had one daughter and a young son as the total pool of labor for a house and farm of thirty acres, plus a dairy herd and three horses. This, it should be noted, was in a day before electricity, running water, and powered machinery were available on the Manchester farm. As such, Stephen almost always employed at least one farm hand. There was no dearth of potential labor, especially given the strong influx of immigrants into the area. It appears that Stephen desired to employ one or more live-in workers whom he could count on to help operate the farm. However, he had trouble doing so. Rather, he ended up with hands who would stay a week or month and then move on. Some did so because they had no roots in the area. Others may have had a drinking problem or, for one reason or another, just did not want to settle in one place. In addition, there is evidence that Stephen was a man of some temper, and his level of pay was sometimes in dispute as being too low. While there is no way to tell why the situation was such, in the fall of 1892, not long before his divorce proceedings began, Stephen did not have a full-time employee.

About 5:00 in the afternoon on a day in late October or early November, Stephen was cutting green barley. A man approached him and asked in broken English, "Job for me?" Stephen asked the man if he knew how to milk a cow; the man said he did. Stephen told the man he would try him, and the man pitched in cutting the barley. Finishing that, the two men fed the cattle, did the chores, and milked the cows. They then ate supper and went to bed, with the man sleeping in an upstairs Manchester bedroom.

The next morning, the hired man arose early and did the chores, but abruptly left the farm about 6 o'clock. Stephen apparently did not know why the man left, but he did not return.

Six months later, on a day in mid-May of 1893, Stephen was milking his cows when the same man came into the barn, with his coat draped over his arm, and asked him again, "Work for me?" Stephen gave the man a pail and he began to milk a cow. The man stayed for supper and boarded in the upstairs bedroom. The next morning, Stephen, as usual, started on his milk route at 7 o'clock. The man, later identified as Jose Correiro, a recent immigrant from the Azores, accompanied him on the cart. They finished the route and returned home about 1:30. The two men then planted potatoes. Again, Correiro stayed overnight. He accompanied Stephen on his milk route on the next two days.

On this third day, however, things changed. At about 11 o'clock, the pair were at South Main Street and Charity Lane when Correiro spotted two Portuguese and approached them. Manchester continued alone on his route. Upon returning to where the men were still congregated, one of them flagged down Manchester. Apparently, this man was also from the Azores, but he spoke English. While Manchester was gone, Correiro had told this man about his work on the farm. The man asked Manchester what he intended to pay Correiro for his efforts. Manchester told him that Correiro was "green," and did not speak English. However, he was a good milker. Manchester said he was willing to pay $15 per month, plus room and board. The man told Manchester that Correiro would not accept less than $20 per month. Manchester told him he would not pay that amount to an inexperienced worker. In addition, he had to point to something when he wanted "Manuel," as he referred to him, to do anything. Thus, Correiro could not work independently, as he could not comprehend a set of instructions. The conversation ended there, with Correiro not getting back on the milk cart. Manchester never saw the two strangers again.

Two days after the conversation on the Fall River sidewalk, at about 3:30, Manchester was in his field along Wilson Road planting potatoes with a Frenchman he had hired, whom he called George. (Like the Borden sisters, Manchester did not seem to have much interest in learning his employees' real names, at least if they were foreign.) Jose Correiro approached him, carrying a small bag, "such as the Portuguese are often seen to carry their clothes in." Since Correiro had left Manchester during the milk route, he had left some items on the farm. Manchester asked if he had come back for them; Correiro nodded. Correiro also had left before being paid, so Manchester gave him one dollar for two-day's work. Later, Manchester said that, upon leaving, Correiro seemed "cheerful" as he headed toward Wilson Road.

Two days after that, while on his route, Stephen stopped at Mackenzie & Winslow's grain store at 33 Pleasant Street, between Second and Third. Upon exiting the store, Stephen saw Correiro leaning against the wagon with Freddie.

> My boy said: 'Pa, why don't you hire Manuel?' (That is the name we knew him by.) I said: "What's the use? He comes in one door and goes out the other. He's no good to me.' (*BG, Extra*, June 22, 1893)

Freddie persisted with his entreaty and Stephen relented. Correiro had walked away, but Stephen called out to him. Of course, Stephen recalled the earlier conversation with the man on the sidewalk about the rate of pay issue. Therefore, the working arrangements had to be cleared up:

> He took me in Sherer's store [nearby, at 67 Pleasant], where Isaac Barnard acted as interpreter. He finally agreed to come with me [for $15 a month.] We drove home, and he helped me with the work that afternoon and slept in the house that night. He left early the next morning and I didn't see him again. (*BG, Extra*, June 22, 1893)

Almost directly across New Boston Road lived the Manchester's nearest neighbors, the Reed family. Bertha Manchester did not leave the farm often, even to visit neighbors. However, she was aware that Charles Reed and one of his daughters were ill. Therefore, on Monday, May 29, Bertha crossed the road to visit with another of Reed's daughters, Ellen. The murders of Andrew and Abby Borden on August 4, 1892, were amongst the most important events ever occurring in Fall River. The trial of Lizzie Borden for the commission of these murders was to begin in New Bedford on Monday, June 5, so interest in the case again rose to a fever pitch around Fall River. After Ellen updated Bertha on the condition of the Reed family, the conversation drifted to that of the Borden murders. Ellen Reed later told a reporter that Bertha said reading about the crimes made her shudder. In short order, Bertha returned home.

Tuesday, May 30, was Memorial Day. But, being a dairy farmer, it was just another workday for Stephen: milk the cows and deliver 150 quarts of milk. He had hired a boy of about fifteen, John Tonsall, to help in farm duties. Stephen and John got up at 4 a.m. and milked the cows. Young Fred "slept in" until 6 o'clock. Bertha made breakfast. She told her father she was going to make gingerbread that day. Although not stated by Stephen or Fred, later newspaper accounts claimed Stephen asked Bertha to instead join them in their trip to the city, so that she could watch the parade or even participate in the holiday festivities. Bertha, however, was an introspective young woman and, besides, with no help she had a great many duties to perform by herself.

As usual, at 7:30 on the morning of May 30, Stephen left on his milk route, accompanied by John and Fred. Bertha remained at home. As they departed the farm, Stephen saw Bertha at the doorstep.

After having been on the route for a few hours, Stephen looked at the clock on the American Printing Company in Fall River, at the corner of Anawan and Water Streets. It read 11:00. He said to his two helpers, "We have got just one hour to finish the route." Going south from there, they crossed the bridge over Crab Pond. At the south end of the bridge, Stephen happened to see Jose Correiro. "As I met the fellow he leaned his head to one side, and smiled, but I had no talk with him."

The three continued with the route. The last stop was 35 Globe Street, about twenty blocks south of downtown. At 12:30, Stephen stopped at his sister's house. (That he stopped at his "sister's" house comes from newspaper reports. He probably stopped at his "sisters'" house. Lucannah and Mary Manchester lived together at 128 South Main Street. He would have to go by there to go home, and it was close to his next stop.) Leaving there, he went up South Main Street to the corner of Borden. A man named Peckham from Little Compton, Rhode Island, was on the corner selling flowers. Stephen bought $1.50's worth of potted plants for Bertha, which was a considerable purchase in 1893, if one considers Stephen was willing to pay Jose Correiro $15 for an entire month's work. The specific reason for the purchase is unclear, but it may have had to do with the fact that this holiday was originally known as Decoration Day, with the tradition of placing flowers at the headstones of veterans. It may also have been in acknowledgment of Bertha's having stayed home to work rather than join the holiday festivities.

Having purchased the flowers, at about 12:50, Manchester went to Joseph Cadieux's blacksmith shop at 276 Pleasant Street to purchase some grain.

Stephen's business in the city was now done for the day. He made his way to Oak Grove Avenue and drove north to his house. He later estimated he arrived at his house between 2:30 and 2:45. He later told the police and reporters what happened next. There are no police records as to this, so it is impossible to know exactly what he told them versus what the newspapers reported.

Freddie got off the wagon and went into the house to get something to eat. John Tonsall opened the barn door and Stephen drove the horse in. Just as Manchester got inside the barn, Freddie came out of the house yelling that Bertha had been killed.

For some reason, the descriptions of what Stephen Manchester then did differ dramatically.

> The *Boston Globe* claimed Stephen did not then enter the house:
>> After Freddie had told me Bertha was dead, I went to the barn and fed the horse. It didn't take two minutes. (June 22, 1893)
>
> The *Fall River Daily Globe* agreed:
>> [Freddie Manchester said he] ran out and said, "Bertha's been killed." We hitched the horse to a lighter wagon and went for the police. Father did not go into the house at all." (May 31, 1893)
>
>> The writer [reporter] saw the father at 5 o'clock, and he said he had not yet seen the body of Bertha. (May 31, 1893)
>
>> "We hitched the horse to a lighter wagon and went for the police. Father did not go into the house at all." (Freddie Manchester statement to *Globe* reporter.)
>
> But the *Daily Herald* reported things differently:
>> Mr. Manchester hurried to the kitchen, and there he saw the same shocking sight that had terrified his 12-year-old boy. He rushed into his barn, took his wagon and drove rapidly to the city, leaving the two boys at the farm. (May 31, 1893)

As did the *Daily Evening News*:

> Mr. Manchester hurried to the kitchen. There he saw the same horror that had shocked his boy. He felt the girl's body. It was cold and stiff. He hurried through the adjoining rooms, found his daughter's room in a scene of confusion and hurried back. (May 31, 1893)

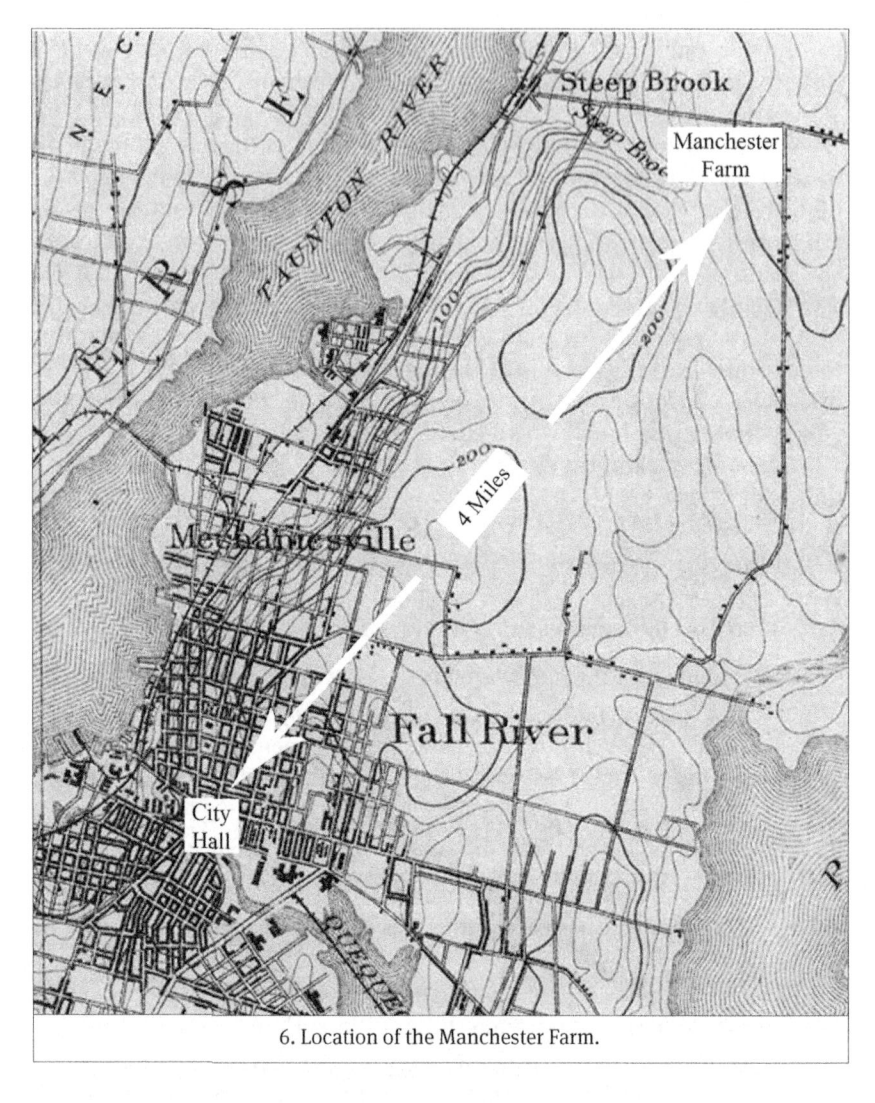

6. Location of the Manchester Farm.

Certainly, the last version would make the most sense from a humanity standpoint. But most reports agreed with the first two versions.

Whatever was the case, there were again differing descriptions of what ensued. One source says that Stephen used the same horse, another that he used a different horse. But there is agreement that whichever animal was chosen, it was then harnessed to a light wagon. Stephen set out southward on New Boston Road, leaving Fred and John at the farm.

Before going to summon the police, Manchester stopped at the house of one of his sisters. Nancy Downing, a widow, lived on New Boston Road about a quarter of a mile south of the Manchester farm. He told her that Bertha had been killed and asked her to go to his farm. As it happened, Nancy had a visitor from Providence that day, her sixteen-year-old nephew, Edward. Stephen then left the Downing house to get the police, and Nancy and her nephew went to the Manchester farm.

The *Fall River Daily Globe* claimed that, after leaving his sister's house, Manchester met George C. Silsbury on the road and informed him of the murder. (The *Daily Herald* agreed.) However, Silsbury worked and lived in the downtown area, so it is unclear as to how Manchester would have encountered Silsbury or why he would have specifically stopped to inform him of the murders. (Silsbury managed a store at 97 South Main. Manchester could have encountered him if he went to inform his sisters Mary and Lucannah, who lived at 128 South Main. Of course, if this was the case, it was after he went to the police station and not before.)

At 2:47, Manchester arrived at the police patrol station on Rock Street. Newspaper accounts claim he spoke to Officers Charles Coggeshall who, in turn, called the Central Station. According to the *Boston Globe*:

> Contrary to common reports, Mr. Manchester did not return immediately to his home on notifying police. He drove on and notified his two sisters, and then went to his son-in-law's residence and notified them.
>
> When he entered the latter residence he was very pale and hardly able to talk connectedly. Then he returned to the house.
>
> [Bertha's] sister, Jennie, on hearing the news, fainted. She is utterly prostrated, and refuses to talk on the subject. (May 31, 1893)

The Bordens happened to have been murdered on the day of the policemen's holiday, August 4. On that day, many of the department had boarded a ship in Fall River and sailed to Rocky Point, Rhode Island, for a day of recreation. There continues to be debate as to whether this coincidence had any effect on the murder investigation, although a study of the case indicates it is unlikely.

On May 30, 1893, Fall River arguably had its second most infamous murder, and, once again, the police force was not operating normally. Because it was a holiday, there were many public gatherings, and many of the police had been assigned to cover them. It would be assumed some others had been given the day off. To complicate matters further, the Borden trial was to begin in a week. The prosecution was putting together its final details. Thus, Marshal Rufus Hilliard was in conference with the prosecution attorneys, Hosea Knowlton and William Moody. However, there is disagreement as to where the meeting took place. One paper claims the trio were at the Central Station; others said that it was in the mayor's office or elsewhere and Hilliard had to be summoned by Captain Philip Harrington. One source claimed that Hilliard then dispatched Harrington and Officers John Ellsbree and George Ferguson to the murder scene.

According to the *Fall River Daily Globe*:

> It was then nine minutes past 3 o'clock. A general alarm was sent into all the stations, officers who were on duty at the Academy of Music and other public places were called in and a large force headed by Inspectors Feeney, Wordell and Medley hastened to New Boston Road. (May 31, 1893)

Assistant Marshall John Fleet was one of those at the Academy of Music. Fleet was born in England in 1848 and arrived in the United States with his family in 1860. On July 7, 1864, at age eighteen, he joined the U.S. Navy and was assigned to the *Scotia*, a so-called ninety-day gunboat, launched in 1861. On April 14, 1865, the day of Lincoln's assassination, the *Scotia* struck a mine in Mobile harbor and sank. Six sailors died and six others were wounded. It is unclear if Fleet was still assigned to the vessel at that time, although it is known that he did suffer a broken arm during his tour of duty.

Fleet left the Navy in October of 1865. Now a member of the Grand Army of the Republic, he was attending their gathering at the Academy. He was thus in his G.A.R. attire rather than his police uniform when he got word to proceed to the Manchester farm.

A call was also made to Dr. William Dolan, the county medical examiner. Dolan telephoned civil engineer Thomas Kieran and photographer Stiff. (There were two photographers named Stiff in Fall River, Fred and James. Each had a studio downtown. Which of the two was summoned is not stated. Dolan had used James A. Walsh to photograph the Borden bodies but, for some reason, used a different photographer this time, although that may have been for the simple reason of immediate availability.)

According to the *Daily News*:

> [J]ust as the assistant marshal was ready [Dr. Dolan] appeared driving fast down South Main street. Assistant Marshal Fleet jumped in with the medical examiner and they started for New Boston Road. (May 31)

Although Dolan and Fleet hurried toward the Manchester farm:

> Neither of the officials knew where the house was, further than that it was near the Wilson road. Nearly at the end of the same road they came upon three boys standing in front of a house. Asking if they knew where the Manchester farm was they were informed that they were in front of it. The assistant marshal asked if there had been a murder there and the boys said yes, one of them proceeding to explain. There were then no neighbors in sight, and everything was quiet about the house. (*FRDEN*, May 31, 1893)

THE MANCHESTER HOMESTEAD.

7. The Manchester House — Front View. From the *Fall River Daily Herald*, June 1, 1893.

Dolan and Fleet encountered two large dogs. A female mastiff was chained in a kennel near the cellar entrance. A Newfoundland was untethered. He was old and toothless but commenced a ferocious bark.

Of course, the concept of a police car was far in the future. The police thus had to employ a different method of getting to the distant Manchester farm as quickly as possible:

> Inspector Wordell was sent from the police headquarters to the Academy to call the officers there, and then with Inspectors Feeney and Medley and Officers Mayhall and Reagan, 2d, took possession of a wagon and started after Assistant Marshal Fleet

and the medical examiner. Captain Harrington went out in a buggy and behind him was the patrol wagon with a load of officers. (*FRDEN*, May 31)

Other stations were called. Policemen on night duty were summoned to the station and sent to the farm by patrol wagon. By 4 o'clock, there were twenty police officers at the Manchester property.

8. The Manchester House — Rear View. From the *Boston Globe*, June 1, 1893.

Somehow, the newspaper reporters learned about the murders. Many were covering or watching a holiday baseball game in the city. Word apparently spread amongst them, and they were immediately off to the farm.

The *Fall River Daily Herald* stated:

> The police began searching within two minutes after their arrival. There were Assistant Marshall Fleet, Inspectors Wordell, Medley and Feeney, Captains Desmond, Doherty, Harrington and Connors, and Patrolmen Ferguson, Coggeshell, Elsbree, Hoar, Mayhall, McAdams, Reagan, 2nd, Davol, Hyde, Wilson and other who cannot be recalled on the moment. (May 31, 1893)

Some officers were assigned to search the property and surrounding woods. The higher-ranking officers and some other policemen went into the house:

> The north kitchen door, upon being opened by Dr. Dolan and

Assistant Marshal Fleet and Captain Harrington, presented a most horrible sight.

On the floor lay Bertha Manchester dead. Dr. Dolan felt of the body. It was cold, and he announced that she had probably been dead six or seven hours. (*FRDG*, May 31, 1893)

In the Borden murder case, Dolan was chastised by the defense at trial regarding his estimates of times of death. They got Dolan to admit he used no thermometer to take accurate body temperatures; Dolan countered with the claim that he was very adept at sensing body temperature to within a degree or two merely by touch. It would certainly seem, in Bertha's case, that no thermometer was needed, since after six or seven hours even a layman would be able to tell her body was at room temperature.

EXTERIOR OF THE ELL.
9. The Manchester House — Kitchen Ell and Well House. From the *Fall River Daily Globe*, May 31, 1893.

It would seem Dolan got to the Manchester farm at about 3:30. This would mean the estimated time of death was 8:30 – 9:30 that morning:

> She wore a calico dress of turkey red with a white figure not unlike a mussel shell upon it. A skirt of dark navy blue calico with a white figure of two interlocking Os, a cambric apron of

blue and white, the checks in double lines. The clothes were badly disarranged and wound up in each other, and it was only by close examination that the garments could be identified, except the waist. The drawers were exposed at the waist and were buttoned. There were black stocking and inexpensive and worn shoes upon her feet. No outrage of person had been committed if one was attempted. (*FRDEN*, May 31, 1893)

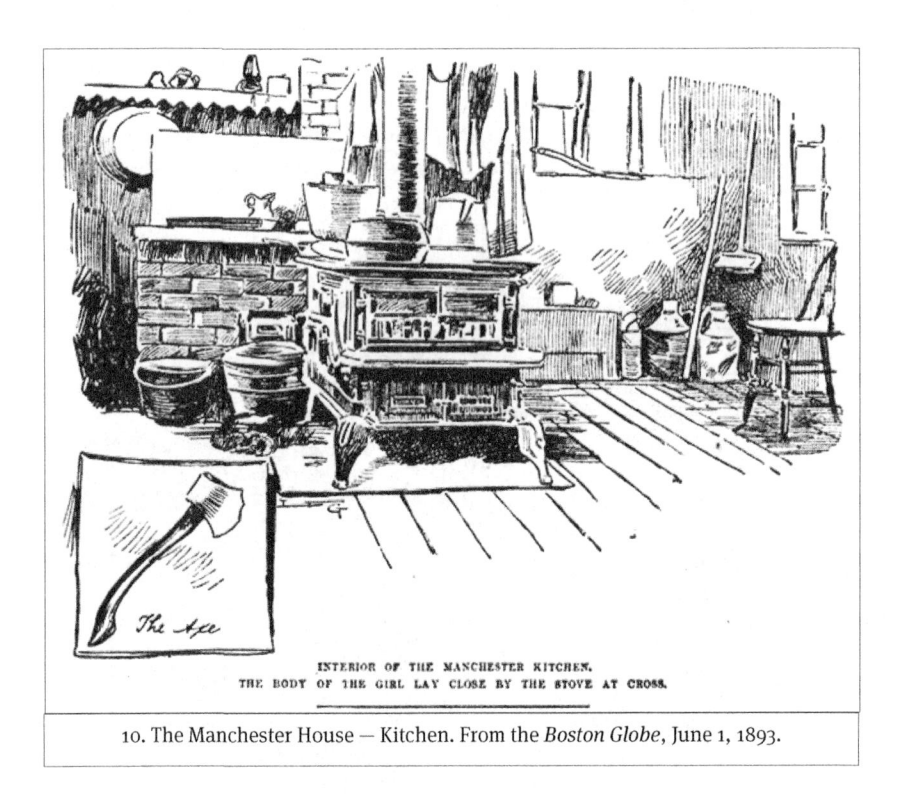

INTERIOR OF THE MANCHESTER KITCHEN.
THE BODY OF THE GIRL LAY CLOSE BY THE STOVE AT CROSS.

10. The Manchester House — Kitchen. From the *Boston Globe*, June 1, 1893.

Those studying the Borden case often comment on the ghastliness of the wounds. The scene at the Manchester house was, if anything, worse:

> The remains lay next to the stove, and between that and the door. The woman lay on her right side. Her right arm clutched a mass of light brown hair, half of which was dyed in blood, and her left was under her body. She lay with her right leg drawn up under her, and resting on it. Her clothes had been pulled down or torn from her hips and the left leg was exposed from the knee. One cut was straight across her neck, about two and one-half inches long, another was half an inch above, and a third an inch above that. The top and back part of the girl's head was badly crushed and cut most horribly.

A gash was found on the girl's lips, and her nose looked as though it had come in contact with some blunt weapon and had been crushed or flattened. From appearances, it was evident that an axe had been wielded with terrible effect, and possibly a stone or flat blunt object had also been used. Great pools of blood lay under the girl's head, and at her feet, and between the stove and the window next to the door, were two large clots, and their position and appearance indicate if anything that there had been a struggle, and a hard one. The wounds were evidently deep ones, and from a half to 2-1/2 inches long. A cut two inches long on the girl's forehead was an ugly one. (*FRDG*, May 31, 1893)

11. The Crime Scene. From the *Fall River Daily Globe*, June 1, 1893.

Andrew Borden had been attacked as he lay on the sofa. The first hatchet blow, at the least, incapacitated him. Abby Borden survived the first blow, but subsequently fell where she had stood. Since both of victims died almost instantly, blood loss, except for some spatter, was confined to the areas under the heads of the bodies. The struggle between Bertha Manchester and her attacker was prolonged, however, and not confined to one spot:

> The bleeding had been profuse. It extended from her head, in a strip about a foot wide without diminishing until it was lost

under the body. It was still bright at 6 o'clock, but coagulation had taken place to a considerable extent. The top looked like thick blood, but by putting one's finger into it the lower part was watery and left no stain on the finger. The stream had appreciable depth and was apparently an eighth of an inch or more through. Behind the body ran a stream about an inch in width, prevented from spreading by the coal hod that stood behind and in line with the north side of the stove. In a semi-circle beyond the feet of the girl were smooches of blood three feet or more in diameter, that looked as if they might have been made by the girl's dragging herself on the floor. (*FRDH*, May 31, 1893)

The *Fall River Daily Evening News* added:

The wounds were even more repulsive than their horrible show of blood. The face had been smashed, cutting through the lips and crushing the nose. Two teeth were knocked out and lay on the floor a foot or more from the girl's mouth and beside her body. There was a cut two inches long on the forehead. One on the back of and across the neck, 2-1/2 inches in length. Another two inches above this, and still another slightly above. The back of the head was crushed into a soft jelly. (May 31, 1893)

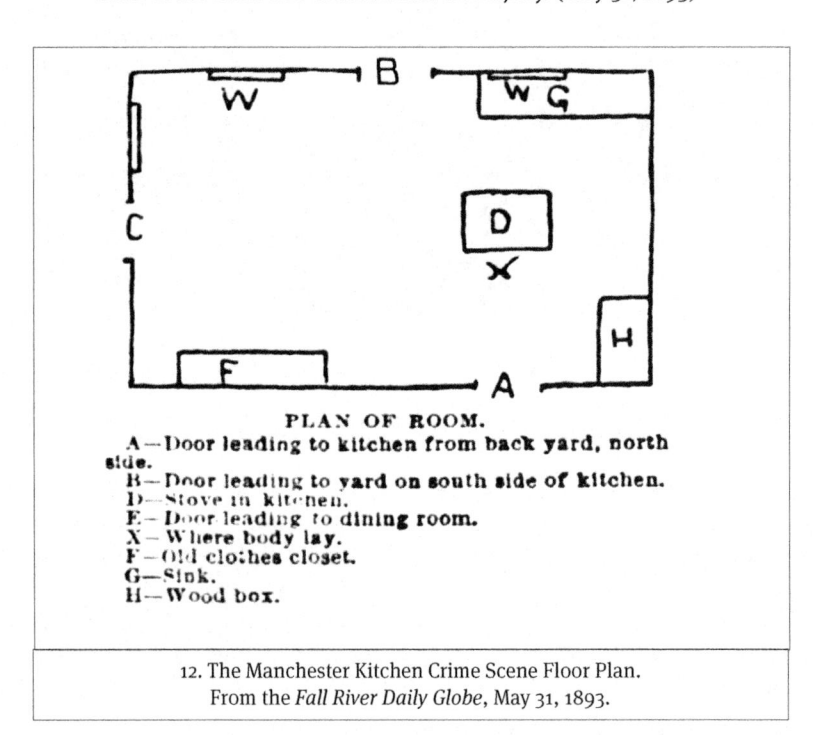

PLAN OF ROOM.
A—Door leading to kitchen from back yard, north side.
B—Door leading to yard on south side of kitchen.
D—Stove in kitchen.
E—Door leading to dining room.
X—Where body lay.
F—Old clothes closet.
G—Sink.
H—Wood box.

12. The Manchester Kitchen Crime Scene Floor Plan. From the *Fall River Daily Globe*, May 31, 1893.

The Manchester house was an old one. The kitchen was a small wooden ell, about 10 x 20 feet, at the back end of the house. Behind that was an even smaller well house accessed only by an outside door:

> The kitchen was a typical country kitchen, full of rubbish and household utensils. In one corner stood an unused clothes press, in another a sink and on the west end of the room was built an old brick chimney and brick oven. The stove reached within a foot and a half of the north door and some chairs and milk cans lay in the corner opposite, and near the exit to the south yard. Still another door led from the kitchen to the dining room. (*FRDG*, May 31, 1893)

What the culprit expected to find is unknown, but clearly Bertha was in the kitchen when the struggle ensued:

> The kitchen showed that Bertha had been cooking when the murder occurred. Pans lay on the stove, and tins with gingerbread dough in them were placed near two vessels full of milk. (*FRDG*, May 31, 1893)

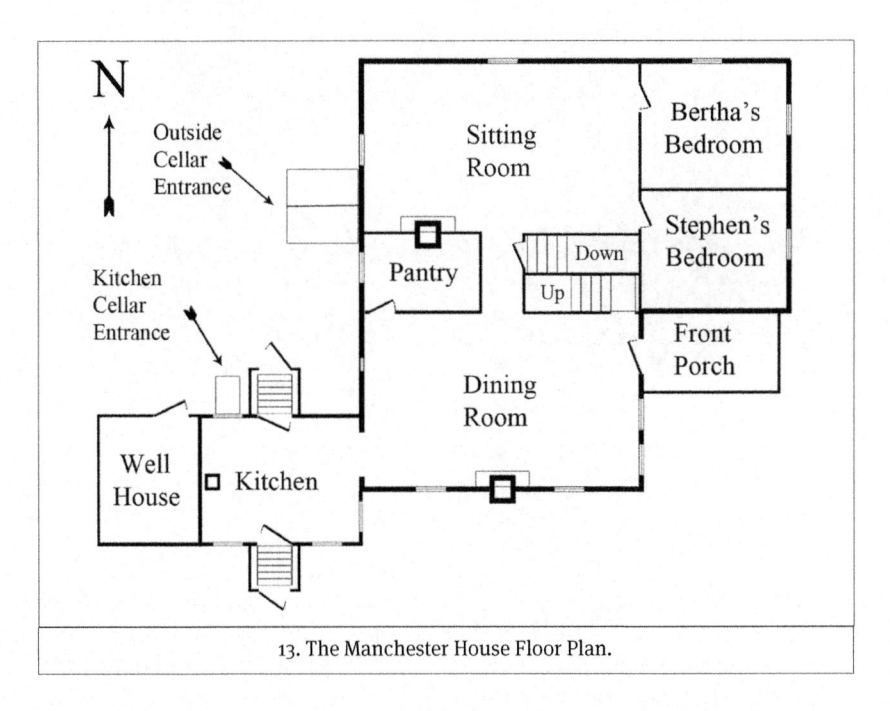

13. The Manchester House Floor Plan.

The front portion of the Manchester house ran north and south. The kitchen ell projected to the west from that. The ell had entry doors on both the north and south sides.

The violence of the attack was further indicated by other evidence:

> On the window opposite the north side of the stove, according to Officer George Ferguson, there were 77 spots of blood, on the sill 5, on the sheathing beneath, 150, in the space 25 x 26 inches, on the stove, 50, on the door 43. (*FRDEN*, May 31, 1893)

Engineer Kieran took measurements and Photographer Stiff took views in the house scene from several vantage points.

THE WOOD PILE.

14. The Manchester House Wood Pile. From the *Fall River Daily Globe*, June 1, 1893.

The Borden case was greatly hampered by the lack of physical evidence. If one discounts the handleless hatchet that was later shown not to be the murder weapon, there was not one clear piece of evidence found by police. They did not fare much better in this one. In the yard, Officer Charles Hoar quickly discovered an axe sitting on a woodpile about twenty feet from the house. Given the nature of Bertha's wounds, this was immediately suspected as being the murder weapon. Stephen Manchester confirmed it was his axe. It was easy to identify – shortly after purchasing it, Manchester broke of part of the blade while cutting wood. Now clearly useless for that purpose, the axe was then relegated to kitchen duty. It was kept in a wood box near the stove and used for chopping kindling.

Once given the run of the house upon the police completing their work, a *Fall River Daily Herald* reporter took it upon himself to thoroughly inspect the axe:

> The axe was the ordinary kind used by woodsmen, perhaps smaller, if anything, and had not been used a great deal, although a large piece had been knocked from the blade. Its length was 27¼ inches. The blade was 3½ inches in width, its length being 7 inches. Blood had been wiped from the instrument, the tracks of the cloth being plainly visible. Blade and handle were stained with blood and there were many hairs on the head where it had been used in smashing in the skull. The axe was usually kept in the kitchen wood box, and Mr. Manchester thinks it was in the wood box when he left for the city in the morning. (May 31, 1893)

15. Path to Rear of Manchester Farm. From the *Fall River Daily Herald*, June 1, 1893.

But even assuming this was the murder weapon, it did the police little good. Fingerprinting was in its infancy, and not employed yet in Fall River.

And, given the nascence of the science, there was no fingerprint record to refer to anyway.

Another officer went into the cellar below the kitchen. He found a rock, about 12 x 5 inches, stained with blood and spattering, on some barrels. This led him to an initial feeling that the attack somehow started there, or that the rock was a murder weapon. But further investigation showed that blood had dripped through the floor of the kitchen. Some of it hit the rock, and then spattered on the barrels.

There was a blood-covered stick found outside the cellar door and an old scoop shovel was placed over it.

Unfortunately for them, this is all that was discovered by the police. They had the murder weapon, but not one clue as to who wielded it. Today one might ask about skin, blood, or hair evidence possibly left by the perpetrator, but there were no such tests available in 1893. Had Bertha torn off a piece of shirt, say, that might have helped, but it was not to be.

The door on the east side of the kitchen led to the dining room and a pantry:

> The officers found the dining table uncleaned, the remains of breakfast upon it. In the pantry was a pan of gingerbread, all the stiffening not yet stirred in. Pans of milk set for cream, unskimmed, with other dishes and eatables, lined the shelves. (*FRDEN*, May 31, 1893)

A passageway from the dining room led to the sitting room, which remained in good order. Off that room was Bertha's bedroom:

> There is no carpet on the floor, but the bed had been made. With the exception of the bed, nothing could be more disorderly. Drawers had been pulled out and ransacked, closets opened, a trunk emptied and its contents added to the litter of the floor. Some of the things had been thrown upon the bed, others upon the chair and all was confusion. The shutters were closed, and entrance must have been made in some other part of the house. (*FRDEN*, May 31, 1893)

Upon speaking with Stephen Manchester, the search of the bedroom revealed new clues:

> Some cheap jewelry was among the articles that were strewn about, but a $50 gold watch with a gold cable chain, a present to the girl from her father two years ago - he gave a silver service to another daughter at the same time - was missing. Several purses were found, some of them entirely empty, others containing a few pennies, a total, if we are rightly informed, of eleven. The girl's father says that she had at least $10 in money to his knowledge, and her brother-in-law states that she always kept some money in her purse and usually in the small purse, which was one of the empty ones. Upon her clothing the only

articles found were a pocket knife and two handkerchiefs. (*FRDEN*, May 31, 1893)

But there was some evidence the murderer had been in somewhat of a hurry to collect his booty:

> In this bedroom there stood a bureau or dressing case, on top of which was a plush box, the receptacle for a watch.
>
> It had formerly contained Miss Manchester's gold watch, valued at $50, but the timepiece was missing. The case stood open. Near its side stood a triangular jewel box, made of pieces of glass, and trimmed with ribbons as a young girl would make during her leisure hours.
>
> It contained a woman's silver watch, a number of gold rings and also several gold pins. This jewel box was in plain view of anyone who entered the room, but its contents were intact. Nothing had been molested. This circumstance is considered rather strange, for if robbery was the motive for the murder it is singular that the jewelry was not taken. (*FRDG*, May 31, 1893)

The upstairs rooms were found to be less tidy than those downstairs, but there was no evidence anything was taken from there.

When Dr. Dolan allowed reporters the opportunity to enter and observe the state of the house (thus affording the detailed descriptions given here), he and Assistant Marshal Fleet had little to tell them about the crime other than the finding of the axe. After about half an hour, Dolan expelled them from the house.

At around five o'clock, Dolan sent word to the undertaking parlor of Daniel D. Sullivan & Son of 115 South Main Street to come to the Manchester house and remove Bertha's body. It would have to be assumed, given there was no telephone service in the area of the Manchester house, that Dolan dispatched an officer to either find a telephone and contact Sullivan or go to the parlor directly. It is unknown if the officer reported back to Dolan, but, by six o'clock, the undertaker had not yet shown. At this point, Dolan told the Manchester family of the arrangements. This caused great consternation to Stephen Manchester and his sister Almira. (Eventually, Nancy, Delaney, and Almira had made their way to the Manchester house, as did Manchester's daughter Jennie and her husband, W. W. Coolidge.)

> [Manchester] yelled and made such a fuss that Captain Connors had to use force to keep him from the kitchen. The women cried and expostulated. Manchester broke away, shook his fist, and talked louder than ever, but there was no appeal from Dr. Dolan's decision, however, Capt. Connors suddenly opened the door, as Manchester opened it after him, after breaking in, and reached out a double barrelled shot gun. (*FRDG*, May 31, 1893)

As for Almira:

> [H]is sister . . . piteously pleaded for the retention of the body, and to be allowed to call Dr. Dwelly to examine it, and who at the same time held that the medical examiner had no right to prevent her from doing her pleasure in this matter. (*FRDEN*, May 31, 1893)

> Mr. Manchester and Mrs. Terry were sent back into the other room and the door was forcibly shut upon them. They were still firm in their protest, however, and referred to the decapitation of several persons by Dr. Dolan in an accusatory manner. Mrs. Terry came at least once afterward to the kitchen door and looked sorrowfully upon the dead girl. (*FRDEN*, May 31, 1893)

Mrs. Terry's concerns date back to the Borden murders. Note the following from an article that was summarizing Dr. Dolan's testimony at Lizzie Borden's preliminary hearing, nine months before Bertha's murder:

> The skulls were removed from the body [sic] by instruction of the attorney-general. The skulls were cleaned and the bodies are now buried without the heads.

> The skulls were photographed and they are now in my possession. No member of the Borden family was informed of the removing and photographing of the skulls as far as witness knew. (*FRDG*, August 26, 1892)

Thus, it was general knowledge after their murders that the skulls of Abby and Andrew Borden had been removed from the bodies.

That Dolan "decapitated several persons" may have been from town gossip. While looking at the case broadly and in a historical perspective, there would have been no reason for Dolan to have kept Bertha's skull for forensic reasons, it is certainly understandable that the Manchesters had no way of knowing this at the time, especially under the conditions of the moment.

Dr. Dolan was adamant that the body must be removed, as it was his duty to do so. Assistant Marshal Fleet reassured the family that Dolan was correct. The Sullivan wagon arrived at about 8 o'clock and the body was collected:

> The red calico dress which was wrapped around the mutilated body was dripping with blood, and the blue apron was also soaked. (*FRDG*, May 31, 1893)

Dolan now made a second objectionable decree: The Manchesters were to vacate the house for the night:

> Manchester objected profanely. Up to this time he had shown an indifference to matters about him which astonished those who noticed it. It was said that even after the crime was discovered

by his son, he fed his horse before changing his rigs to notify the police. (*FRDG*, May 31, 1893)

Manchester said he needed to boil water to clean his milk cans, as cows had to be milked and deliveries prepared for. His pleadings were in vain.

William W. Coolidge, Manchester's son-in-law, seemed to perceive that Stephen was seen unfairly as being cold-hearted. He spoke to reporters to set the record straight:

> "Mr. Manchester thought the world of Bertha. She was a hard worker naturally, and her father gave her the management of the place when he was away. It is a shame to say that he was indifferent at her death. You ought to have seen him after the police left. He had been dazed at the terrible affair and up to the time when he was called into the house by the police at 6 o'clock, he had stood about the yard not knowing what to do. His thoughts turned, naturally to his cows which needed milking. The police would not let us heat any water and the cans had to be washed in cold water. I had to carry up supper to him because they could not build a fire in the stove." (*FRDH*, May 31, 1893)

Memorial Day, 1893, had dawned on a positive note for most. For the Manchesters, it looked like it would be just another day. They had not participated in the holiday festivities, but at least they would have gingerbread for dessert that night. But by day's end:

> The old man and two boys camped in the barn, and the women went to their respective homes. Among those who were in the house were Mrs. Delaney Manchester, Mrs. Downing, sisters of Mr. Manchester, and Mrs. W. W. Coolidge, a daughter of the latter. (*FRDG*, May 31, 1893)

> Officers Ferguson and Wilson were detailed for guard duty at the house during the night, and the family were ordered to provide themselves quarters elsewhere. (*FRDEN*, May 31, 1893)

Dolan, Fleet, and the other police officers made their way back to town:

> After 10 o'clock there was a consultation in the marshal's private office, in which Mayor Coughlin, Marshal Hilliard, Assistant Marshal Fleet, Captain Desmond and Captain Doherty took part. The murder was discussed in every aspect, but the outcome of the conclusion reached, if one was reached, was kept secret. From certain movements of the police it is thought that their suspicions have become fixed upon some definite person as the murderer, or inciter of the murder. Those suspicions arose more from general impressions than from any clue that has been discovered. Whether or not there is any foundation for the suspicions of the police will be definitely determined before another day passes. It there is not, then the murder will continue as great a mystery as it now seems. (*FRDEN*, May 31, 1893)

CHAPTER 4
THE INVESTIGATION BEGINS

May 31, 1893

The autopsy commenced at 10 o'clock on the morning after the murder. It was performed at the funeral parlor of Daniel D. Sullivan & Son at 115 South Main, where the body had been delivered the previous evening, as this was before the time when Fall River had a dedicated cadaver storage facility. Dr. Dolan was assisted by Drs. George Eddy, Herbert Wilbur, and Dwight Cone.

Bertha was found to have been in fine physical health before the attack. Twenty-three distinct head wounds were discovered. It is difficult to see how the doctors were able to determine this many individual wounds with a skull so crushed. Most of the wounds were on the back of the skull, and five pieces of bone were extracted. There were at least two wounds on the front. The first was a triangular one on the forehead. The second extended from the chin to the nose. This blow knocked out five teeth. The thorough search of the kitchen revealed only two teeth, which were now in the possession of Dolan. One is thus forced to deduce Bertha swallowed the other three.

It would not take a medical professional to determine the cause of Bertha's death. But, of course, the autopsy was necessary for additional reasons. Had the autopsy revealed sexual assault or pregnancy, the possible motive for the crime would have been expanded beyond a simple burglary having gone bad. Bertha's autopsy indicated neither situation.

On the day of their murders, the stomachs of Andrew and Abby Borden had been removed and sent to Dr. Edward S. Wood at Harvard University. An element of the Borden case was that the couple might have been poisoned, but this suspicion did not arise until after the stomachs had been removed. Rather, the procedure was conducted to help establish the times of their deaths. This was not necessary in the case of Andrew, as the time of death was certain within a few minutes. But the time of Abby's murder was of utmost importance in solving the crime. Since it was known the two had eaten breakfast at the same time, a comparison of the state of digestion had been useful in establishing when Abby met her fate.

As to Abby Borden's time of death, police already knew it had to have been between 9 o'clock, when she was last seen, and just after 11 o'clock, when Lizzie Borden returned to the house from the back yard and any possible intruder had left the premises. There was a much broader window for Bertha Manchester. She was last seen about 7:30 in the morning, when the men left to do the milk route. Freddie Manchester discovered Bertha's body upon returning about 2:30. The advanced state of blood coagulation and low body temperature gave Dolan a good idea of how long she had been dead, but analysis of the stomach contents would afford one more piece to the puzzle. As such, Bertha's stomach was removed and sent to Dr. Wood.

In the case of the Borden murders, the police began suspecting Lizzie Borden almost immediately, although they were never able to gather sufficient evidence to prove her guilt to a jury. The Manchester murder was essentially the opposite situation. Clearly, no family member was involved, but the evidence at hand indicated that a former employee of Stephen's was the culprit. This was based on the dogs apparently not barking (although it must be said the neighbors were somewhat detuned to noticing this) and that an employee would be knowledgeable of the Manchester house, its occupants, and their habits. There had also been rumors in the city that Stephen kept a sizable quantity of cash in the house, although this was untrue, at least at the time of the robbery.

If a former employee was the culprit, it allowed the police to focus on the usual suspects – immigrants of the lower classes:

> They are fully convinced that a former employe [sic] of Mr. Manchester killed the girl. With this idea in view they found trace of a suspicious character, a Portuguese named Manuel Carreiro, and the last man who was employed by Mr. Manchester.
>
> He is described as a man about 22 years old, small of stature, with black hair, clean face except a small black moustache, and a comparative stranger in the city. He worked three days on the farm, last week or the week before, and left because of the manner in which he was treated by the old gentlemen.
>
> Carreiro came to America from the Western Islands about two months ago and went to board with a distant relative, Jacinto Muniz, who lives in the middle tenement of the eastern row of the Narragansett mill blocks. Muniz [whose full name was Jacintho Muniz Machado] is a mill operative and also conducts a band of Portuguese musicians. (*FRDG*, June 1, 1893)

We see that, within a day, the *Globe* was claiming that Manuel Carreiro, whose name we have previously seen was actually Jose Correiro, was suspected by police. This is interesting in two ways. First, Stephen had told police on the day of the murders that he did not suspect any of his former employees. He admitted he had somewhat contentious relationships with most of them but thought none of these situations rose to the level of someone invading his house. But even if Stephen had suspected a former employee, he told the police that he kept records only of first names. If he did not know the man's actual given name, he would make up a nickname. In the case of Correiro, Stephen called him "Manuel," so, even if he thought Correiro could have been involved with the crime, he had no way to identify the man to the police. Manchester told reporters that his record book had been taken by his daughter Jennie after the murder and had subsequently been handed over to the police.

Manchester's providing the name "Manuel" was little to go on. But old-fashioned police work led them to Correiro. Either by looking at the record book, or just going on the fact that Manuel spoke no English, the police deduced "Manuel" was a Portuguese. They further knew that a man named Isaac Barnard was often approached by Portuguese new to the city, inquiring of him if he knew of anyone who might be hiring labor. The police had quickly interviewed the man and found it was he who had sent Jose Correiro to the Manchester farm.

Although the police learned Corriero's identity, they did not find him. After leaving the Manchester farm:

> Carreiro returned to the city and located at the residence of Manuel Peters [Frank Peter] on Eagle Street. The police also learn that he left Peters' place early Tuesday morning, saying that he was getting up to the Narragansett blocks to get his truck and that he intended to go to Newport. He expected to get employment at some farm house in the vicinity of that city. (*FRDG*, June 1, 1893)

The police could find no one who had seen Correiro since he left Peter's house. At this point, Correiro was no more than a person of interest. He had been the last Manchester employee and his sudden disappearance called for an explanation.

The June 1 issue of the *Fall River Daily Globe* included a startling event:

> The [funeral parlor] has been visited by scores today who desired to look at the bruised and cut face of the murdered girl.
>
> Most of the visitors were women. Before turning to look through the glass plate that is placed directly over the face, the morbidly curious female would shut her eyes and draw her frame up with a deep inward breath and then look, shudder and make some remark indicative of terror and pity.

> The dark brown hair on the dead girl's head is combed back straight. On the left side, and just an inch from the forehead, is a peculiar gash, that apparently was made by the perfect corner of the axe blade. Its deepest part is towards the centre of the head, and is merely a surface scratch on the edge nearest the forehead. This wound is an inch long, and a quarter of an inch deep in the deepest place. (June 1, 1893)

The morning after the murders, Stephen Manchester left on his milk route in the usual manner. He received much criticism by many Fall River residents for doing so. How could a man return to his typical daily duties less than one day after he found his daughter brutally murdered?

> He did not cry out or show signs of great grief, and for this reason many were ready to hold him subject to suspicion. He is a hard, stern man, complete master of himself, and not one to show emotion. (*FRDEN*, June 1. 1893)

The *Boston Globe* made the most outrageous statement regarding Manchester's demeanor:

> The murderer may have had a desire for revenge on the old man for some past grievance, but if such was the case and he wreaked vengeance by killing the daughter the murderer fell short in his object, for the old man does not worry about the loss of his daughter. (June 1, 1893)

However, his sister Nancy Downing and his son-in-law said that they, as relatives, could see the grief displayed in his demeanor.

Further, as we have seen, Stephen Manchester was not one who might have been considered a typical man. First, he was a dairy farmer, a man who had to work every day. As the *Daily Evening News* put it:

> An old sea captain, Mr. Manchester had always been accustomed to go ahead with his work, no matter what happened. He was a whaler for 20 years, sailing out of New Bedford and Fall River, and in that time must have been compelled to go on with his work in the face of disaster and possibly tragedies. Much criticism has been offered because of the trouble that he had in milking his cows and caring for the milk. The cows had to be milked and there was no one to do the work but he and the green chore boy. (June 1, 1893)

In addition, he had not even been allowed to enter his house at this point.

Often overlooked in this matter is the condition of the cows. Consider the following, from the website unbottled.com:

> [I]f a cow goes too long without being milked, milk will build up in her udder, causing it to become full. This will cause her to become uncomfortable. This doesn't happen with the normal amount of time between milkings. If a cow, who was in the

middle of her lactation and producing eight gallons of milk per day, went for a significant time without being milked, it could cause bruising, udder injury, sickness and, if it continued, could result in death (this would take many consecutive days without milking).

As a dairy farmer, Stephen Manchester relied on his animals, and he probably did not want his cows to go a day or more without being milked. But also consider that each of his scores of customers needed milk daily. In short, Stephen Manchester probably better contended with his grief by following his daily ritual than if he had sat idly for hours in his barn.

The police had thoroughly searched the small house on the afternoon and evening of the murders, but the restrictions on entry remained on Wednesday:

> The Manchester house was the scene of interest for newspaper men yesterday. In the morning the house was kept closed and no one except officers were admitted. The reporters could walk all over the farm and look at the outside of the house from every point of view, talk to the neighbors and do about everything they please except the two or three things they wanted to do. Officers Fred Barker and Mark Shay were on guard at the doors, and no one except officers could enter without the permission of Medical Examiner Dolan. (*FRDEN*, June 1, 1893)

After completing the autopsy, Dolan returned to the Manchester house, followed by Engineer Kieran and Dr. Cone. When Stephen, Freddie, and John Tonsall returned from their milk delivery, once again they were disallowed entry into the house. Dolan did allow the reporters access to the house, but they discovered nothing they had not found on the previous day. However, sketch artists were now present as well and began making illustrations of the house and property.

By now, Boston reporters had shown up and Dolan patiently brought them up to speed on the case. According to the *Fall River Daily Herald*:

> The Boston newspapers are represented by many of the same men who came down for work on the Borden case. Among them are George H. Brennan and Mr. Wood of the Boston Herald, John Carberry of the Globe, Mr. Archer of the Journal and several sketchers and assistants. (June 1, 1893)

In the search for printable material, the reporters were forced to seek out the observations and opinions of the Manchester's neighbors. However, unlike the Bordens' neighborhood, the houses here were widely spaced and thus there were only a few who could be considered neighbors.

They interviewed Richard Reed, who lived about a quarter of a mile south of the Manchesters. He affirmed that Stephen had trouble keeping farm help. One Portuguese told Reed of Manchester:

"'Me no work for Old Starboom, anyhow,' – that's what they call Steve Manchester. They didn't like him. They wern't on the place mor'n a day a few days." (*FRDEN*, June 1, 1893)

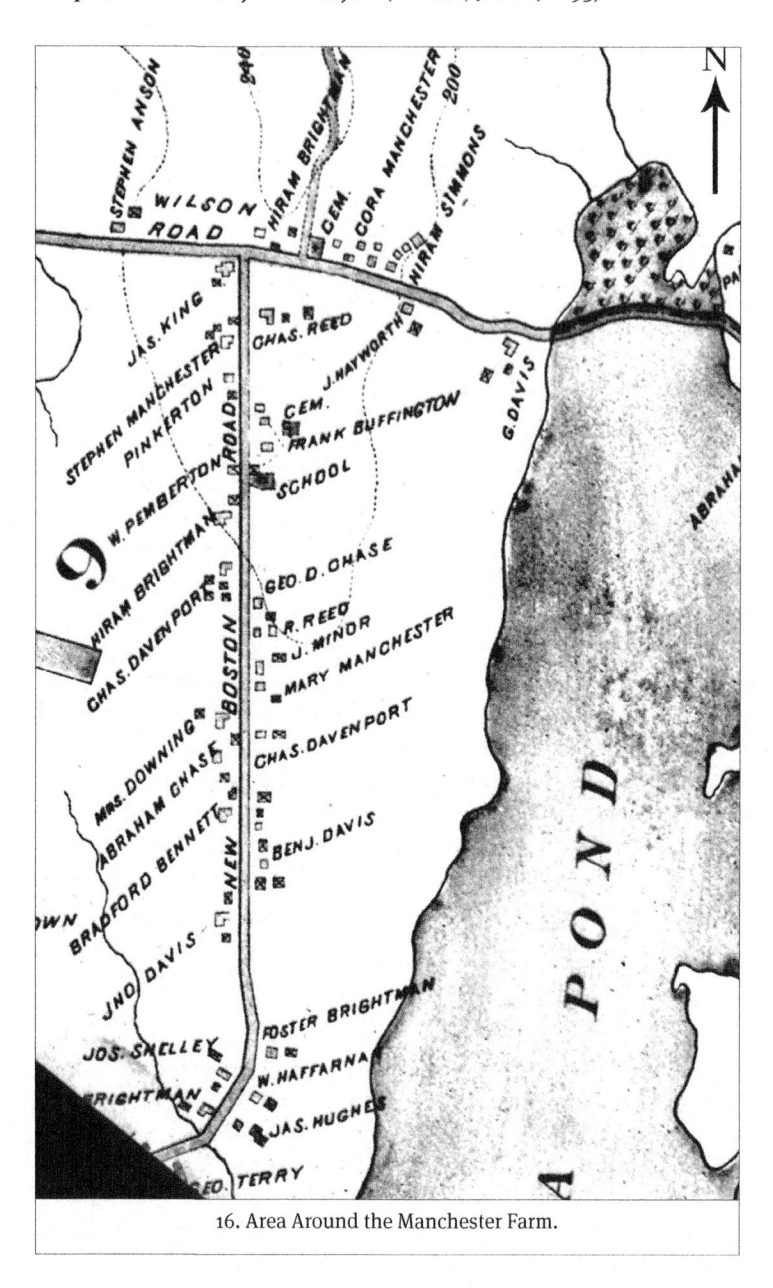

16. Area Around the Manchester Farm.

Ellen Reed was the daughter of Manchester's nearest neighbor, Charles Reed, who was Richard Reed's cousin. She could provide no information regarding the day of the murder, but did have much to say about Bertha, whom she had known since birth. She was a "good girl" who did not attend church, because she had no time to do so. She had a "sweet disposition" and did not complain at the heavy work required of her on the farm. Bertha loved the animals on the farm, especially the horses. She had never had a beau. To the best of Ellen's knowledge, Bertha had nothing to do with the break-up of Stephen's marriage.

Ellen *had* heard one of the dogs bark the morning of the murder but had not paid any attention to it. However, she did not hear the dog bark in the afternoon.

It is interesting how the newspapers covered any similarity between the Manchester and Borden murders.

In Fall River, the *Daily Evening News* did not bring up the issue. The *Fall River Daily Globe* made a list of similarities. But in the end, they conceded:

> [T]he resemblance between the two horrors ends with the time of day, the hatchet, the robbery and the supposition of that a Portuguese farm hand is the guilty person.
>
> There was no double murder on Tuesday, no relative is suspected, no property is involved and there is no weapon to be unearthed. It was a brutal, clumsy, country murder, prompted by one of two motives. Perhaps murder was not intended originally. Certainly the preparations for it were crude. The premises furnished the axe and the stone. If lust or avarice drove the wretch to the farm, he may have reasoned that he could carry out his ends without killing, and realizing his mistake, save himself by felling the woman whom he assaulted. (May 31, 1893)

The *Daily Herald* came to the same conclusion:

> Much is being said in the newspapers about the similarity of the Manchester and Borden murders and the respects in which the murders present like conditions. They were all committed in the light of day and the instrument used in both cases was an axe. The victims were hit about the head in all cases.
>
> Beyond those it is not possible to go. The Bordens were old people living on one of the principal streets of the city. Bertha Manchester was young, living in a lonely farming district. The Bordens were stricken down in their own homes, but at times two hours apart. Their house was occupied by one or more persons at the time of the murders and the discovery of the deaths was within 20 minutes of the time when one of them took place.
>
> Bertha Manchester was stricken down in her own home where she, with the murderer, was the sole occupant, and it was at

least five hours after the murder when a police authority looked on the stricken form. (June 1, 1893)

The big-city *Boston Globe* took a much different approach. They saw almost nothing but similarities. These stretched to the point of, frankly, ridiculousness:

> Andrew J. Borden was wealthy, so is Stephen C. Manchester, father of the murdered girl. His is not so rich as the Borden estate amounted to, but among farmers he is considered among the wealthiest in Fall River's farming territory.

> Mr. Borden was close, penurious and exacting and overbearing. These are also Stephen Manchester's chief characteristics. (May 31, 1893)

On the evening of May 31, the Boston paper took it upon itself to interview Lizzie Borden's lawyer, Andrew J. Jennings. This interview made sense, said the *Globe*, because:

> Since this morning, when the comparisons were made by THE GLOBE of these two tragedies, the opinion has become rife that there is an extreme probability of their being made a feature by the defence in the Borden trial, which begins at New Bedford on Monday. (June 1, 1893)

Jennings, who had just returned from Boston after working on the Borden defense, told the *Globe* that, given his circumstance, he had little time to acquaint himself with the details of the Manchester murder. The *Globe* reporter kept egging Jennings to declare similarities in the crimes. Jennings kept refusing to do so, with responses like, "You fellows ought to be able to form your own deductions from these things. You know more about this than I." These vague answers cause the *Globe* to conclude:

> The attorney's reply is sufficient itself in character to admit of a pretty confident conclusion that he will use these analogous circumstances in Lizzie Borden's defence. (June 1, 1893)

The reporting differences here are quite remarkable. The hometown papers approached the Manchester–Borden comparison in a matter-of-fact manner. The illustrious Boston paper reported the connection like a tabloid. While the reason for this cannot be discerned, it is noteworthy that the previous autumn the *Boston Globe* had issued false reports on the Borden case, based the work of its reporter, Henry Trickey. Private detective Edwin McHenry had been employed by Marshal Hilliard to help in the Borden case investigation. Trickey offered a bribe to McHenry to reveal evidence in the case. McHenry told Hilliard of this, and false documents were prepared to trap Trickey, who turned the documents over to his employer. The *Boston Globe* immediately published their contents without checking with any sources or even conducting perfunctory research, such as referring to the *Fall River City Directory* to check names and addresses.

Within a day, the *Boston Globe* discovered its error and was in serious trouble. Certainly, they could have been sued by Lizzie Borden and, far worse, their reputation as a newspaper had been jeopardized. They quickly issued a retraction and an apology. But one wonders if, from that point forward, they wished to do everything they could to be on the side of Lizzie Borden. And, clearly, suggesting the two cases were intertwined was very much in Lizzie's favor.

Certainly, the police saw no connection in the crimes:

> Wednesday night Marshal Hilliard caught time to answer a few questions put by a HERALD reporter regarding this latest crime, and his words will prove reassuring to the public. He said he could not understand why there should be talk of a mystery in connection with the horrible murder of the innocent Manchester girl. No one could doubt the motive of the murder.
>
> The girl's old father himself showed what the cause of the murder was. Her money and watch were missing, and her position when found indicated that she struggled for her honor and for her life. It is idle to think of the old man as the murderer of his daughter. The officers satisfied themselves of this fact after examining the boys and the old man collectively and separately. (*FRDH*, June 1, 1893)

Hilliard went on:

> "[The Borden and Manchester murders are] not similar," he replied. "Here there is a motive, possibly two motives for murder. In the other case there was no robbery, no rape, not even the slightest shadow of a motive for hours, and we were all at sea. At Manchester's we were on the scene first, but the poor victim had been dead for hours. At Borden's we were on the scene early, but we were not the first who were there, and one at least of the victims had been dead only a short time." (*FRDH*, June 1, 1893)

Hilliard noted the anomaly that when the Bordens were killed many of his policemen were at their annual outing in Rocky Point while, on the day Bertha was murdered, many of the people in the Manchester neighborhood had gone downtown to participate in the Memorial Day festivities.

W. W. Coolidge apprised the police that it had been determined that seven dollars had been taken from Bertha's bureau.

June 1, 1893

On Thursday, June 1, the police made little additional progress. Jose Correiro was still their main suspect, although there was not one shred of evidence against him. It was merely that he had been a recent employee of Stephen Manchester before the murder. He was focused on because of his mysterious disappearance after the murders and, one might suppose, because the police could not come up with anyone else to look for. While Stephen Manchester admitted some friction between himself and Correiro, the same could be said regarding most of his previous employees.

The police had little chance of finding Correiro without the help of the Portuguese community of Fall River, as can seen in the following:

> Carreiro last boarded with Frank Peters, a well-known Portuguese on Eagle street, and left the house Tuesday morning, about 9 o'clock. He was going, he said, to the house of a cousin in the Narragansett mill blocks to get his clothes. He intended to go down on the Island of Rhode Island, he said, to look for work on a farm. He did not go for his clothes, and they are at the home of his cousin in the Narragansett mill blocks now awaiting him. The Portuguese in the mill blocks are inclined to keep any knowledge which they may have of Carreiro to themselves. They have given to the police some information about him, but they do not talk readily to them. It is a known certainty that Carreiro lived not long before he went to the Manchester farm with his cousin [Jacintho Muniz Machado, familiarly known as Jacinto Muniz]. (*FRDH*, June 2, 1893)

However, on Thursday, Officer Martin Feeney successfully enlisted Frank Peter to accompany him to Tiverton, Rhode Island, the north side of which borders on the south side of Fall River. The fish factories there were known to often employ the Portuguese. Although it might seem strange that a Portuguese would help look for Correiro in Tiverton with Feeney, if it could be shown Correiro was there the morning of the murders, he would be exonerated. And, if they could not find any record of him there, nothing was made worse for Correiro.

Visits to several factories in Tiverton resulted in only one substantial lead. A man at Brightman & Brown's factory said he had spoken with two men at noon on the day of the murders. He knew this was the time, because he was speaking with them just as the 12:00 dinner whistle blew. He told them there was no work there for them. One of the men matched the description of Jose Correiro. If this were him, it was almost impossible for him to have committed the murders.

Peter told the police that Correiro had left at about 9:00 on the morning of the murders. Correiro told Peter he was going to Jacinto Muniz's house in the northwest part of the city to get his trunk. The newspapers disagreed as to whether Correiro actually went to the Muniz house:

> *FRDG*: As near as the time can be fixed he was at the Bowenville house, where his trunk is, at 9:30, or half an hour after he left the Peter's place.

FRDH: At his boarding house, which is opposite the Weetamoe mills, it was learned that he had called there on Tuesday morning, but staid only a few minutes, and then left, saying he was going up to the farm. He did not take his trunk.

FRDEN: He was going, he said, to the house of a cousin in the Narragansett mill blocks to get his clothes. He intended to go down on the Island of Rhode Island, he said, to look for work on a farm. He did not go for his clothes, and they are at the home of his cousin in the Narragansett mill blocks now awaiting him.

BG: Early Tuesday morning he left the house on Eagle st. and as he bids the family good-by, remarks that he is first going to his relative, Jacinto Muniz' house in the Narragansett block, to get his clothing and other effects. He did not, however, go there, and has not been seen since that time by any of the men who knew him, but his clothes are still at the Muniz' house.

Whether Correiro actually went to the Muniz house is important. The Peter house at 8 Eagle Street was located many blocks west of the downtown area. If Correiro left the Peter house at 9:00 and walked directly to Tiverton, he could easily have arrived there by noon. Making the long walk to the Muniz house in the northwestern part of the city and then walking back south to Tiverton would have been much more difficult within the time frame. Perhaps more to the point, walking north to the Muniz house took him in the direction of the Manchester farm.

If Correiro did kill Bertha Manchester, his being in Tiverton at noon is close to impossible. If he walked directly from the Peter house, it would take him about an hour to get to the Manchester farm. It would take somewhat longer if he first went to the Muniz house. After murdering the girl, he had to clean up sufficiently to be presentable in public. He then had to travel about ten miles south to Tiverton and apply for work at noon and, at some point, had to meet up somehow with the second man.

It was considered that Correiro could have taken the train to Tiverton. Assuming he traveled from the station nearest the Manchester house, at Steep Brook, he had to take the 10:20 train to Tiverton. While this would have gotten him to Tiverton for the noon factory visit, the 10:20 train departure would make it extremely unlikely that Correiro had enough time to get to the Manchester house, commit the murder, clean up, and get to the train station in time. (It should also be said that a person in Correiro's financial circumstance was unlikely to have train fare, unless, of course, he used money stolen from the Manchester farm.)

After visiting the fish factories, Feeney and Peter walked northward back to Fall River, stopping at all the farms along the way. No one interviewed had seen a man fitting Correiro's description.

Peter had discerned the identity of the second man who had applied for work at Brighton's. He lived on Eagle Street in Fall River. Upon visiting that location, Feeney and Peter were informed the man in question had left several days earlier to search for a job.

Officer Charles P. Hoar was one of the men assigned to guard the Manchester property. He took the opportunity to investigate around the farm:

> Officer Hoar, who was searching at the farm house yard yesterday, picked up a piece of woolen drawers on a shrub in the orchard behind the barn.
>
> He found on investigation that it was smeared with blood. A short distance away he found another but smaller piece of the same material, undoubtedly a portion of the larger rag. The smaller remnant had blood on it also.
>
> The find was quickly reported and the fragments of cloth brought to the marshal's office. (*FRDG*, June 2, 1893)

It was discerned the cloth was part of a pair of men's underdrawers. Given the forensic technology of the day, the actual cloth was of little value, short of the police finding the rest of the underwear in someone's possession. It did tend to confirm that the murderer left the Manchester farm via the back yard. However, such an exit route could be deduced using common sense, as the perpetrator would likely have been seen at some point by someone on New Boston Road. Also, there was a small creek behind the farm where the murderer could clean up:

> Chief Hilliard, in talking with a GLOBE man today, said that he rather thought the cloth was an old piece that had been laying in the orchard, and that the murderer's eyes spotted it, as he went between the apple trees; and that he wiped his hands on it. (*FRDG*, June 2, 1893)

Not considered by Hilliard in this statement is that there was no way to determine if the blood smearing was due to someone using the cloth due to a previous farm accident.

Thus, while Officer Hoar's discovery was the only recent clue, it was of very little value.

Although the police were concentrating on Jose Correiro, other leads were also followed. According to the *Fall River Daily Globe*:

> Two young girls told an officer that they had seen the negro in the woods near the water works tower, and that he looked like a suspicious character. (June 2, 1893)

Officers were dispatched and soon found Louis Quarry. He said he had come from Boston and had been in Fall River only a day or two.

The police immediately became suspicious because, besides displaying strange behavior, Quarry said he was originally from Florida, despite the fact he displayed a strong accent typical on the east side of New York City. A search of Quarry revealed a laundry list written in a feminine hand and a clean white linen handkerchief. These were deemed sufficient to hold Quarry while further investigation was conducted. It was discovered that Quarry had been in Fall River for a week.

The Manchester house still remained off-limits to the family. Stephen Manchester had had enough of not being allowed entry to his home while reporters and police came and went and employed attorney A. E. Bragg to get things moving on the issue. Bragg appealed to Marshal Hilliard, saying Manchester had no objection to the police taking anything they felt was evidence, but that he wanted to be back in his house again as he could not even cook a meal. The appeal was in vain, as the order stood.

The city aldermen met and acted in the case:

> "That the Mayor be, and hereby is, instructed and authorized to offer a reward of $500 to any person or persons giving information that will lead to the discovery, apprehension and conviction of the person or persons who murdered Miss Bertha Manchester on the day of May 30." (*FRDG*, June 2, 1893)

At one o'clock on Thursday, two days after the murder, Bertha's body was transported from the Sullivan funeral home to that of Henry Waring & Son at 152 South Main Street. The Manchesters had made the request. Dr. Dolan assured a *Daily News* reporter that the remains were intact, despite some rumors to the contrary.

The family announced that a private funeral would take place at 1:15 on Sunday, June 4, with Bertha then being interred at Oak Grove Cemetery.

Word had gotten to Stephen Manchester's oldest son Harry of the murder of his sister. Harry had been estranged from the family for twelve years and now lived in Quincy, Massachusetts. He arrived in Fall River on the afternoon train and immediately visited the funeral home where his sister's remains lay.

The three daily newspapers of Fall River were fiercely competitive. When one found another to have reported in what appeared to be a less than accurate manner, it would quickly note this in a future edition.

As we have seen, the *Fall River Daily Globe* had reported that Bertha Manchester's body had been on display to the public at the Daniel D. Sullivan & Son funeral parlor. Thinking this was suspect, the *News* asked Sullivan about the claim:

> Undertaker Sullivan says the account is largely overdrawn. There was not a general exhibition of the remains. To a few eminently respectable citizens opportunity was given to view the corpse, but in no sense was it a public exhibition. Examiner

Dolan also has a grievance. He declined to state the number of wounds inflicted, but says the number reported, 23, was correct. He feels sure none of the surgeons who assisted reported the fact and says the report must have been given by an employe [sic] of the establishment. Dr. Dolan urges the necessity of a morgue, where such operations can be conducted in privacy. (*FRDEN*, June 2, 1893)

Given the *Globe* story and that the initial Borden autopsies had been performed in the family's sitting room, Dolan's request was not unreasonable.

JUNE 2, 1893

Louis Quarry was brought to the Central Station and arraigned in court before Judge John McDonough on a charge of vagrancy. He pleaded "not guilty." Assistant Marshal Fleet asked that the prisoner be held until it could be determined if he had committed a serious crime. McDonough agreed to this and continued the case until the following Tuesday. He was ordered to be held on a $500 bond.

The police dispatched a large detail of officers to the east-west section of New Boston Road, to the west of where the road turns to the north. Two teams of three officers were instructed to beat the brush northward, toward the Manchester farm. Captain Connors, who had dropped off these officers, continued driving with additional officers to the Manchester farm, where they performed an intensive search of the house. They also dragged the well in the Manchester yard as well as another behind the barn. Finishing these tasks, the group searched the orchards and fields behind the barn. They then searched the properties southward until they met up with the northbound teams.

The only possible clue found during this search was of a red piece of cloth, discovered about half a mile southwest of the Manchester farm. For some reason, the newspapers could not agree as to its description:

FRDG: Officers Skelly and Bassett found a handkerchief yesterday, while searching the woods, but the spot on it was not blood.

FRDH: A piece of bloodstained red bandana [was] picked up by Officer Skelly.

FRDEN: A close examination made it clear that there were no blood stains on the handkerchief and it had been lying out in the woods for some time, having been wet by the rain at least once.

BG: Officer Skelly picked up two pieces of cloth. . . . They were blood-stained parts of handkerchiefs.

The medical examiner was finally through with his work in the

Manchester house:

> Early in the afternoon, Dr. Dolan ordered a window sash sent to the Manchester home, and expected the new one would be substituted for one having the blood-stained panes on it. The window arrived but since the doctor was not present, the change was not allowed to be made.
>
> Later, Dr. Dolan himself had the work done under his supervision. The glass with the red spots on it, now has a place with the other relics at the medical examiner's home. (*FRDG*, June 3, 1893)

Much to the relief of Stephen Manchester and his son, after removal of the window, Dolan turned over the house to its owner.

The police were convinced that the finding of Bertha Manchester's watch would lead them to her killer. Marshal Hilliard sent the following, via telegram and printed cards, to police chiefs in New England:

> A lady's gold hunting case chased watch, Waltham movement, No. 2,377,280; also a gold chain, rope pattern, tow strand, with slide; chain attached to watch; the letters "B.M.M" on the outside of the case. The watch was taken from the house, and at the time when Bertha Manchester was murdered, on Tuesday, May 30, 1893. If found, please wire at once. (Signed)

R. B. Hilliard, City Marshal, Fall River, Mass., June 2, 1893

June 3, 1893

The police had quickly focused on Jose Correiro as not only the main person of interest, but the only identified person of interest. The newspapers had reported extensively on the search for Correiro, but now, after three days, their patience was running thin. After all, "the police continue to search for Jose Correiro" does not fill much space nor pique the reader's interest. As a result, the papers began significant coverage on other possible suspects.

Unfortunately, other than Louis Quarry, no one had been arrested in Fall River. This forced the newspapers to report on suspicious people over a broader area. Identified were:

- A suspicious Portuguese man in the northern part of New Bedford.
- A man who applied for work at the Wakefield Rattan Company but quit after working just three hours.
- A man named Will Davis, who recently escaped from an insane asylum. The *Fall River Daily Globe* claimed Davis worked for Stephen Manchester in 1888.

- A darkly-complected man with a scratched face who was seen walking on the Taunton turnpike.
- A tramp in Newport who spoke with an Irish brogue.
- A Portuguese arrested in Barre, Vermont.

But the newspapers were making a broader allegation: these and other leads were being followed up because, although they still wanted to find him, the police no longer felt Correiro was their man.

The *Fall River Daily Globe* quoted Marshal Hilliard as saying, "while we think that Correiro must be captured to satisfy ourselves and the public, still we are looking elsewhere for a suspected perpetrator" (June 3, 1893).

The *Daily Evening News* went further:

> There is now reason to believe that the Carreiro clue will be dropped as soon as it has been worked out. It was the most plausible thing that offered itself, and the police have worked it faithfully until they have reached a point where they are beginning to believe that Jose Carreiro is not the man they wanted after all. (June 3, 1893)

The Associated Press was even more assertive:

> It has been definitely determined by the police that Jose Carreiro is not the man wanted for the Manchester murder.
>
> The police practically arrived at this conclusion last night, but were unable to give it out officially until this forenoon. (*BG*, June 3, 1893)

But the time had come for some crow to be eaten by the newspapers. At 7:00 that night, Jose Correiro turned himself in to the Fall River central police station.

Jose Correiro did not come to the police station alone. He was accompanied by his uncle, Jacinto Muniz, and Portuguese community leader Frank M. Silvia, who spoke English.

Correiro's appearance was not unanticipated by the police. Somehow Silvia found out that Correiro was in Taunton. At 4:30 in the afternoon, Silvia gave this information to Captain Philip Harrington. The police contacted Muniz and told him to produce Correiro by 7 o'clock, or they would arrest him (Muniz) by midnight:

> When Carreiro came to this city Saturday night he did not expect he would have to answer for the murder. He had been hoodwinked. His friends and uncle, Jacinto Muniz, and Carreiro himself, thought he was here to tell about a certain man who had stolen a horse on Tuesday morning. Inspector Feeney put up the job, in connection with his colleagues, Medley and Wordell. (*FRDEN*, June 5, 1893)

17. Police Searches on June 2, 1893.

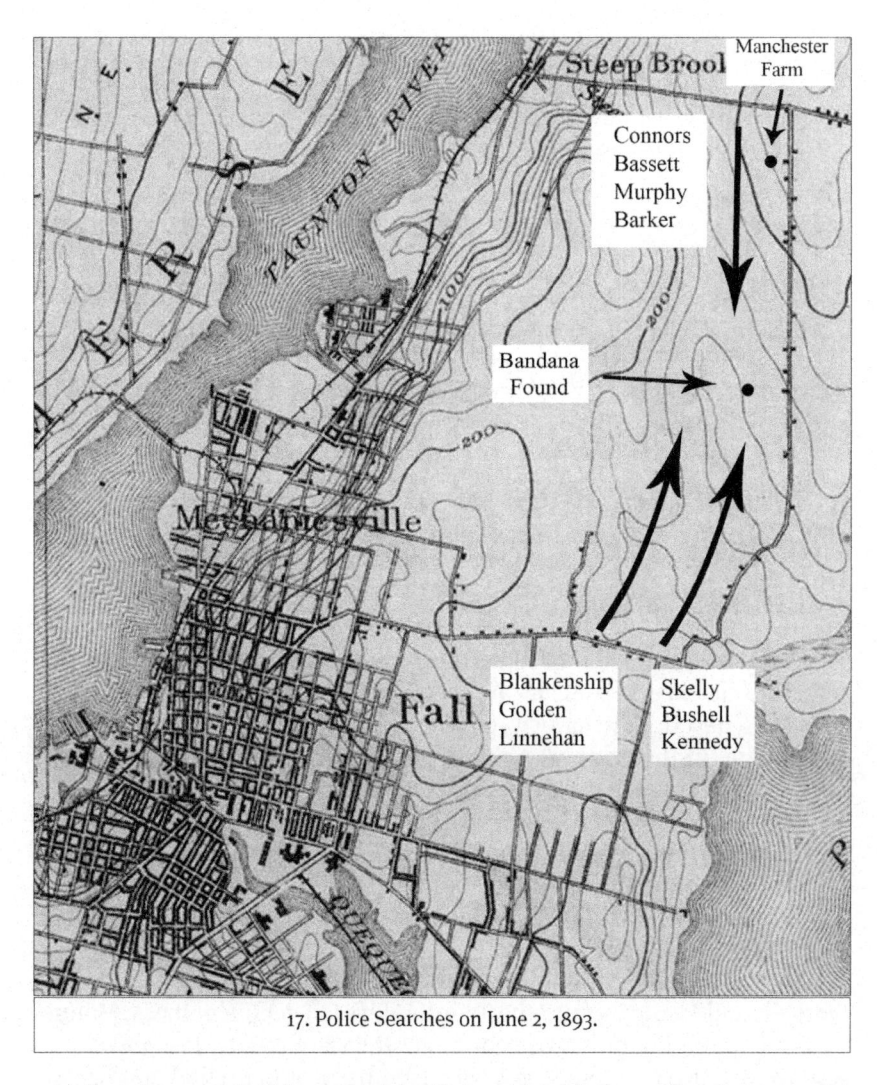

Correiro was in his early twenties and told the police he came to the country ten months earlier. He said he was unaware the police were looking for him until he spoke to Muniz that day.

The *Fall River Daily News* reported that upon Correiro's being brought into the station by Muniz, many policemen, plus Marshal Hilliard, Assistant Marshal Fleet, and Mayor Coughlin, were brought in for his interview.

Edward W. Murphy, the mayor's private secretary, made a stenographic report of the interview:

> Silvia as interpreter gave the following account of the suspect; on Memorial Day Carreiro arose at 7 o'clock and went to the house of Frank Peters, where he ate breakfast. He says that he spent the greater part of the forenoon following the Portuguese band about the city, and at 11 o'clock went to the Crab Pond bridge where he met Stephen Manchester.
>
> He lifted his hat to Mr. Manchester and the latter nodded to him. He worked a couple of days on the Manchester farm a month ago. Later he fell in with several of his countrymen and boarded the noon train for Taunton, where he was informed he could obtain employment in a brick yard. He had nothing to do in Fall River, and he could not pay his way, his relatives had intimated that he must go to work somewhere. He secured a job in Taunton. (*FRDG*, June 4, 1893)

Correiro claimed that were witnesses who could support this account.

As may be assumed, the police were not accepting Correiro's version of what happened at face value:

> The inspectors were kept going after witnesses, and their drives took them out to the New Boston and Wilson roads and across the river, witnesses being awakened and brought from their beds. (*FRDEN*, June 5, 1893)

The police also knew of something that Correiro did not mention. Just that day, they had become aware that on Memorial Day a man matching Correiro's description had purchased a pair of shoes from a shop in Bowenville, in the northwestern part of the city. Another man had also been in the store at that time.

The police asked Correiro if he had purchased a new pair of shoes on Memorial Day. He said he had. (It would seem likely he was wearing them.) At the store, he had the shoes wrapped in paper. He took them to the Muniz house, after which he put them on, and put his old shoes near the front door.

During the questioning of Correiro, Hilliard sent Inspectors Feeney, Wordell, and Medley across the Taunton River to get the witness, Manuel Sousa. Captain Connors was sent to get the shop owner, Joseph Lacroix, who lived above his store at 364 North Main Street. Correiro had revealed nothing that was incriminating during his questioning, but it was decided to lock him up pending the arrival of Sousa and Lacroix.

18. Jose Correiro. From the *Fall River Daily Herald*, January 8, 1894.

CHAPTER 5
THE ARREST

June 4, 1893

Half an hour after Jose Correiro was put in his cell, Manuel Sousa arrived at the police station, followed shortly thereafter by Joseph Lacroix. They were taken to see Correiro, whereupon both identified him as the person who came into the store on Memorial Day.

After choosing the shoes, Lacroix told Correiro that the price was $1.50. Correiro took out a woman's purse from which he extracted two coins. One was a trade dollar and the other was a plugged fifty-cent piece.

As explanation, the minting of silver trade dollars was authorized by Congress in 1873. Most initially went to China, but within a few years they entered U.S. circulation. In the U.S., they were not considered face-value coins, but rather were worth their weight in silver. Since the price of silver fluctuated, so did the value of the coin.

In the case of the plugged coin, Stephen had drilled a hole toward the top of each of the coins he gave his daughters, allowing the coin to be suspended as a piece of jewelry. Technically, these were known as "holed" coins. In some cases, to attempt to make the coins legal tender once more, the hole would be filled with the same metal as the original. Such coins were called "plugged." Skillful artisans could do this operation seamlessly. Less-than-perfect repairs (sometimes with non-precious metals) were obvious, and the coin remained worthless, hence, "not worth a plugged nickel."

To Correiro, these might have appeared to be normal U.S. coins but, as a merchant, Lacroix was experienced in coinage. In the case of the trade dollar, he told Correiro it was worth only ninety-five cents. Worse yet for Correiro, Lacroix told him the damaged half dollar was worthless.

Correiro then took two quarters out of the purse. He asked Lacroix to accept the trade dollar at face value. If Lacroix would not do so, Correiro said he would have to pay for the purchase with a large bill. Lacroix said he was eager to close the store and go to the races that were to be held that day at Riverside Trotting Park. (The park, opened in 1891, was located a mile north of Steep Brook, the northwesternmost part of Fall River.)

Lacroix did not want to take the time to open his safe to make change. As a result, he accepted the two quarters and the trade dollar for the shoes. Correiro immediately took off his old shoes and put on the new ones. Lacroix put the old shoes in a box and wrapped the package with paper. Correiro took them and exited the store.

WHERE THE SHOES WERE PURCHASED.

19. Lacroix Store, Fall River. From the *Fall River Daily Herald*, June 6, 1893.

Of course, Correiro had already admitted to buying the shoes. But beyond that, the stories of Lacroix and Sousa completely contradicted that of Correiro:

Correiro denied on a second interview which lasted from 2.30 until 4 o'clock this morning, that he even had a pocket book. He denied that there had been any discussion as to the value of a trade dollar. He said that he had no half dollar in his possession, and did not, as Lacroix stated, change his shoes in the store. (*FRDG*, June 4, 1893)

From there, things only got worse for Correiro. The police visited Bertha's sister, Jennie Coolidge. She said that her father had given her and Bertha identical trade dollars some years before. Unfortunately, she could not produce her coin. Because of its fluctuating value, her husband had recently taken the coin to the bank to determine its current value. He then misplaced the coin. She added that, later, Stephen Manchester gave Bertha a half dollar with a hole in it. Bertha kept both coins in a pocketbook.

20. 1878 Trade Dollar.

21. Plugged 1797 Half-Dollar.

It also happened that police had been notified by a farmer named Mosher that he had seen a suspicious character running down Wilson Road about ten o'clock on Memorial Day. Mosher and his hand, a "Frenchman" who had also seen the man, were brought into the station. The farmer identified Correiro as the man he saw on Wilson Road. The Frenchman said Correiro looked just like the man he saw running down the road.

From that point, Correiro's description of his activities on Memorial Day became even more conflicted and the decision was made to charge him with the murder of Bertha Manchester.

WILSON ROAD, ALONG WHICH THE FUGITIVE FLED.

22. Wilson Road. From the *Fall River Daily Herald*, June 5, 1893.

In an effort to manage what was told to the press, at 3:30 city leaders called what today would be termed a press conference:

> At the hour named there were present at the marshal's office Mayor Coughlin, Marshal Hilliard, Inspector Mahoney, seven local newspaper men and a representative from the Boston Globe. Assistant Marshal Fleet came in before the statement was ended. (*FRDEN*, June 5, 1893,)

Mayor Coughlin issued the statement on what had transpired in the last day or so. The *Fall River Daily Globe* reported:

> All that was safe was given and names were, as a rule, suppressed, through a desire to relieve those who had assisted the police in their work from as much future trouble as was possible. (June 5, 1893)

Given this, it would seem likely that Lacroix's name was not mentioned. However, the *Daily Herald* printed the following as to remarks made to the press by Coughlin:

> On the day of the murder, it is alleged that [Correiro] entered a French Canadian shoe dealer's store near the south end of the Sagamore mill, and asked in broken English for a pair of shoes. (June 5, 1893)

Lacroix was undoubtedly the only "French Canadian shoe dealer's store" in the described area, and the local reporters either knew so or soon discerned it.

Now armed with this information, the *Fall River Daily Globe* sent a reporter to Joseph Lacroix's store. Not surprisingly, Lacroix apparently thought the police would keep his identity secret. He expressed concern at this turn of events and refused further comment to the newspaper, other than to say he did not think Correiro was the murderer. Lacroix feared backlash by the Portuguese community, with whom he did significant business.

Lacroix told a reporter from the *Boston Globe* that he had been admonished by the police not to give information to the newspapers about his dealings with Correiro. The reporter tried to get Lacroix to say what time he had left his store for the races. The reporter was aware that the first race had been scheduled to start at 1:00. Lacroix said he walked to the races, which would have taken half an hour. However, Lacroix was non-committal, saying he did not know. It could have been any time after 9:00.

Jacinto Muniz spoke little English and, therefore, could not answer reporters' questions directly:

> Muniz, the uncle of the prisoner, talked to the newspaper men by means of another interpreter. He said Jose was 19 years old, and had been in the country eight months. He worked at various kinds of hard labor until he tried his hand at farming. He had received a burn on his left arm while employed at the hat factory, and this injury, neglected, has seriously interfered with Jose's health. Muniz said that the injury caused Jose to quit work on the Manchester farm. (*FRDEN*, June 5, 1893)

Muniz also thought his nephew to be innocent of the crime. He said Jose told him he followed the Portuguese band "from the North End to the Santo Christo church on Columbia street" on the morning of the murders, and that there were witnesses who would back this story. Later, he boarded the 1:20 train to Taunton, as he had been advised he could find work there:

> Saturday Muniz heard of the whereabouts of his nephew and told Inspector Wordell. Saturday afternoon he went to Taunton and sent a boy to tell Jose he wanted to speak to him. Then Muniz told him of the murder of Miss Manchester. Jose was very much surprised, and when told further that he (Jose) was suspected of the murder, he expressed the desire to come at once to the Fall River police station, and did so in the manner stated. (*FRDEN*, June 5, 1893)

During the day, police continued to follow up on Correiro's story. He had told police that after buying the shoes, he then returned to the Muniz house and put his old shoes near the front door. Captains Doherty and Desmond were dispatched. They thoroughly searched the Muniz house, yard, and surrounding area, finding no trace of the old shoes.

By coincidence, Bertha Manchester was buried the same day Jose Correiro was arrested:

> The funeral of Bertha M. Manchester took place this afternoon at 1:15, from the residence of W. W. Coolidge, at the corner of Quarry street and Stafford Square. The body of the murdered girl rested in a white plush casket, and there was a profusion of flowers.
>
> The services were conducted by Rev. E. B. Jutten of the Baptist Temple, who read appropriate selections from the scripture, and commented briefly on the character of the deceased, and her sad and untimely end.
>
> There were present about thirty relatives and friends of the family, including the Reeds, who live near the Manchester farm, and representatives of the press. A touching scene occurred at the conclusion of the services when Mr. Manchester and his two sons viewed the remains for the last time.
>
> A funeral procession of 15 carriages followed the hearse to Oak Grove cemetery, where the casket was placed in the tomb near the entrance. The bearers were Henry Reed, Arthur Lown, Mitchell Nicholson and Arthur Brown. Henry Waring & Son had charge of the funeral arrangements. (*FRDG*, June 4, 1893)

June 5, 1893

Jose Correiro had been arrested early Sunday morning. Now, on Monday morning, he was to be arraigned before Judge John J. McDonough:

> The scenes about the district court room this morning recalled the sultry days of last August, when the public was similarly agitated on the Borden case. In the alley about the public

entrance to the court room was an immense throng of people, and as soon as the doors were opened a grand rush for seats was made. The crowd soon filled all the available chairs and settees and many were turned away, being refused admission.

The court room, both inside and outside the rails, was packed with lawyers, witnesses and sight seers, and several of the officers who had cases in court, were obliged to occupy seats alongside the prisoner. (*FRDH*, June 5, 1893)

The public now got its first look at the accused man:

Carreiro [*sic*] looks quite boyish in build and his 20 or 22 years of age is only indicated by the faintest suggestion of a moustache and a goatee. He is about 5 feet 7 inches high and weighs about 140 pounds. (*FRDEN*, June 5, 1893)

The *Daily Herald* added:

He was attired in the same clothes which he wore when he surrendered, Saturday evening, consisting of a light coat and a dark vest and pants. He was pale and haggard looking and evidently realized the position in which he was placed. (June 5, 1893)

As Correiro spoke almost no English, Dr. Emanuel Dutra was brought in as an interpreter. Dutra translated the indictment for him and he responded:

"I do not know anything about it." "Guilty or not guilty?" was asked in Portuguese, and he replied: "Not guilty."

He seemed to be high strung nervously as he sat in the dock, Monday morning, his emotion being displayed by a twitching of the muscles of the face and a peculiar glisten in his eyes. Whenever he spoke to the interpreter, however, he showed no hesitation, or tremor in his voice. (*FRDEN*, June 5, 1893)

Assistant Marshal Fleet was handling the case for the prosecution. He asked for a continuance, explaining to McDonough (who had to be already aware of the fact) that many of the officers involved in the case, plus Marshal Hilliard and Hosea Knowlton, were in New Bedford, as the Borden trial was starting at the same time as this hearing. McDonough granted a continuance until June 15.

Since he was charged with a capital offence, Correiro was committed without bail. To his surprise, and over his protests, Manuel Sousa was remanded as a material witness on $2,000 bail. It would be supposed Joseph Lacroix did not suffer this fate because of his ties to the city, whereas Sousa lived across the Taunton River in Somerset. Later that day, Sousa's brother appeared at the police station. He had with him four bankbooks, showing sufficient deposits to cover the bail. Unfortunately, he owned only one of the books. Fleet told him if the other owners appeared at the station, bail would be accepted.

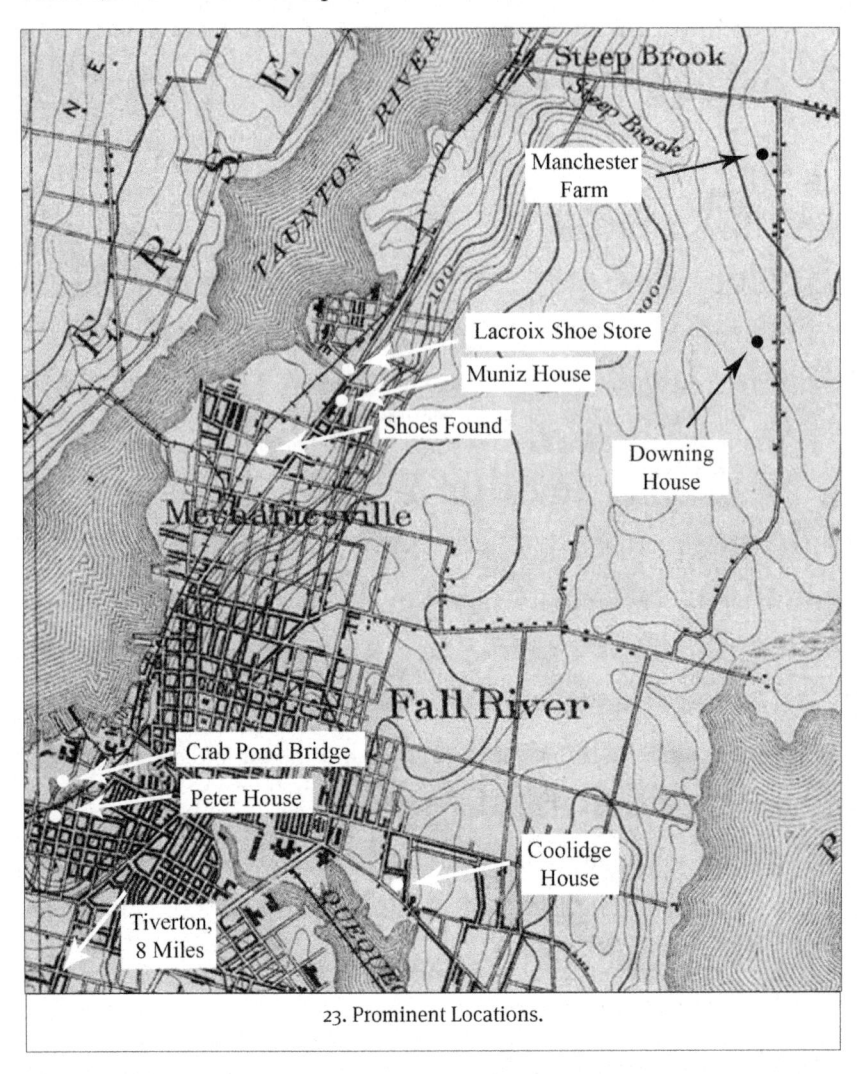

23. Prominent Locations.

Having not found the shoes at the Muniz house, the police contemplated other places Correiro might have discarded them. They considered that upon exiting Lacroix's store, Correiro might have walked around the back of it and traveled along the railroad tracks running north and south just west of North Main Street:

> It was inferred that if the suspect went down the railroad track

and carried the paper box containing his old shoes with him he very likely threw it into some nook or hole.

So it proved. The police had not gone far down the railroad track before they decided to look into the gravel pit on the east side of the track, opposite St. John's cemetery, a short distance north of Brightman street. To their intense gratification there were the objects of their search. They first saw the paste-board box. One shoe was found a few feet away from it and the other had been put inside of an old hut in which lamplighter Thomas King trims his lamps. (*FRDEN*, June 5, 1893)

The police took the shoes to Lacroix, who identified them. He said there also should be a paper wrapping that had been placed around the box. The police returned to the tracks and eventually found the paper, on which was printed Lacroix's name.

While inspecting the old shoes, Lacroix told police it appeared they had been soaked in water. However, the police made no statement as to any possible trace of blood.

When the police found Louis Quarry on June 1, he had acted suspiciously. When brought in for questioning, his story was shaky. They certainly did not have sufficient cause to arrest him for the murder of Bertha Manchester, but he was held on a charge of vagrancy, if only to give police more time to investigate.

When Quarry appeared in district court that morning, Correiro was in the same courtroom and certainly appeared to be the man the police thought to be guilty of the crime. Quarry was off the hook on the serious charge, but not the vagrancy. He pleaded not guilty but was sentenced to one month in the House of Corrections.

CHAPTER 6
THE WAIT

JUNE 6 – JUNE 14, 1893

Now that Jose Correiro was being held for trial, newspaper coverage of the case greatly diminished. This occurred for two reasons. First, Correiro was from an ethnic group commonly considered as likely lawbreakers by the community. In addition to this damnation, from the information released to the press, it certainly appeared he was guilty. But the case would have had reduced coverage in any event because, on June 5, the Borden trial had begun. This higher-profile case would last more than two weeks.

Immediately complicating matters, the *Daily Evening News* printed the following in its coverage of Correiro's arraignment:

> Bail was fixed at $2,000. This sum is regarded as extremely low, and many persons expected that it would be much higher or that the prisoner would not have been admitted bail.
>
> About 2 o'clock this afternoon five friends of Carreiro went to the office of Clerk Leonard, of the second district court, and deposited $2,000 in cash, the amount at which bail was fixed by Judge McDonough this morning. The prisoner was subsequently released. It is understood that a close watch will be kept on him so that he cannot escape. (June 5, 1893)

But, Correiro did not qualify for bail, as he had been charged with a capital crime. Clearly, the newspaper was referring to the bail set for Manuel Sousa, the witness of the shoe purchase.

It is often said, "You can't believe everything you read in the newspaper." While true, the reader has no way of knowing which reporting is accurate and which is not. In Fall River, the sister of Stephen Manchester found herself in such a dilemma. The *Fall River Daily Globe*, one of the two competitors of the *News*, probably enjoyed writing the following article the day after the arraignment:

Jose Correiro is yet confined in a cell at the Central police station, notwithstanding the fact that the news was spread abroad yesterday afternoon that he had been released on $2000 bail, and in the opinion of the police officers of the case, Jose will be a gray-haired man, before he sees the light of freedom again, if that event ever occurs.

There was much unnecessary excitement in the city last night when the false alarm was spread and the authorities were subjected to the severest criticism for allowing such a condition of things to exist.

Within a few minutes after the news had spread, Miss [Mary] Manchester, the eldest sister of Stephen Manchester, came into the Central station in the most excited state of mind.

She leaned over the rail which stands in front of Captain Harrington's desk and gave vent to her feelings between sobs and cries. The captain could not understand the ideas she intended to convey, and as he was ignorant of the lady's identity as well as the fact that the report had been sent out that Correiro was released on bail, he concluded that his visitor was laboring under an hallucination or was a member of the great army of cranks which had before made its influence in these parts. [This referred to the numerous crank letters received in the Borden case.]

Finally he learned that she was an aunt of Bertha Manchester and that her indignation and excitement was due to the false reports which had been circulated. He did not then believe that such a fool story had been printed, but the lady convinced him by flashing a copy of the Daily News and pointing her finger at the announcement.

She declared that such action on the part of the court was an outrage and she told him that she felt sure Correiro and his gang would go direct to the house on New Boston Road and murder her brother Stephen.

It was with some difficulty that the captain succeeded in convincing her that the story was false in every particular and that Correiro was safe behind the bars and no amount of money would be sufficient to effect his release.

The lady thought, and rightly too, that the law did not permit of bail in cases of such magnitude. Captain Harrington told her that she was correctly informed on that score, and he added that such knowledge of the law was so universal that he was surprised that an alleged intelligent man would make the mistake of spreading such a report. Miss Manchester's fears were allayed, and she thanked the captain and withdrew. (*FRDG*, June 6, 1893)

It was reported in the newspapers that the night he was arrested, Correiro was ordered to strip. A spot of blood was discovered "on the bosom of his working shirt" (*FRDG*, June 6, 1893). Correiro admitted it was blood, but was the result of his rubbing a cut on his head and then touching the shirt.

The tight-knitted Fall River Portuguese community rallied around their countryman. Three cousins of Jose Correiro—Manuel Vear, Joseph Siero, and Michael Correiro—called at the Central Police Station on June 6 with clean clothing and food for him, claiming they had heard that such gestures had been made to some previous prisoners. The police refused this gesture, saying Jose had all his needs met. The trio also informed the press that Jose's father, who lived on the Azorean island of St. Michael, had been notified of Jose's plight and had told them he would leave as soon as possible for Fall River. It was believed that the family was of some means, owning two grocery stores and a large farm on the island.

On June 7, the *Boston Globe* reported the Portuguese community also began a fund-raising effort for Correiro, with a goal of $1,000. It was reported that they approached the law firm of Hutchinson, Cummings, and Hutchinson to represent him, but they did not yet have confirmation that the firm would do so. (There was no such firm in Fall River. The newspaper was apparently referring to Cummings and Higginson.)

In an interview with a reporter for the *Fall River Daily Globe*, Stephen Manchester said that he had given Bertha new bills as gifts several times. All bills were of at least two dollars in denomination; some were five. Stephen had given these bills to Bertha to do with as she pleased. However, he had always given her other money for household and personal use, so he supposed she had most or all of these bills at the time of her murder. He did not know where she kept them; he supposed it was in her pocketbook. Manchester acknowledged to the reporter that, at one time, he had kept a substantial sum in a drawer in his house but had since moved it elsewhere. The intruder had searched through the drawers but there was nothing to take.

The *Fall River Daily Globe* claimed to have discovered a new clue. According to the newspaper, before visiting Joseph Lacroix, Correiro "stopped at a house he was well acquainted with." There, he asked a woman to sew up a tear in his coat, which he told her happened while he was walking through the woods. The woman then did so. The *Globe* said it assumed the police were already aware of this clue.

The *Daily Herald* was more circumspect, saying the police had a torn coat "Correiro wore on the day of the murder." But there were only two ways the police could be aware a coat was worn on the day of the murder. The first would be if Correiro admitted so, which obviously was not the case. The second would be if someone in the Portuguese community saw him so attired and identified the coat for the police. As we have seen, no Portuguese was likely to do so. And, even if the latter happened, it should be noted that the police were not giving out information as to any other clues they possessed, so it is difficult to determine how the *Herald* could suddenly be in possession of this information.

On June 8, the *Daily Herald* reported that John W. Cummings (of Cummings and Higginson) had declined the case. Now Nicholas Hatheway was being wooed to that end.

In its coverage of Bertha Manchester's funeral, the *Daily Herald* had written:

> The remains were taken from the hearse, placed in the tomb because the widow of the deceased brother of Mr. Manchester objected to the interment of the body where the husband lies. (June 5, 1893)

A few days later, Bertha was finally laid to rest:

> The body of Bertha M. Manchester was this afternoon taken from the receiving tomb in the Oak Grove cemetery and buried in the lot in the same cemetery which was bought Wednesday by W. W. Coolidge, the brother-in-law of the murdered girl. There were no ceremonies at the grave and none of the relatives were present. (*FRDH*, June 8, 1893)

Given the lack of new information on the case and even more so to the unfolding drama of the Borden trial, the newspapers wrote little about the Manchester case. But, for some reason, the *Daily News* saw fit to send a reporter to Taunton to see if he could discover anything as to the accused's activities there before he returned to Fall River.

The reporter noted that there were "upwards of half a dozen brick manufacturers in Taunton and vicinity" but, eventually, he was able to determine that Correiro had been employed at the Taunton Brick Company. The manager there told the reporter that Correiro's employment began at 6 a.m. on Wednesday, May 31, and ended at 3 o'clock on Saturday, when a "messenger came to the yard from his uncle." Correiro's clothing was "neat and orderly," but he was not particularly industrious regarding the shoveling job he was given, being subject to periods of stopping "to cast his eyes around the yard and in different directions, and especially if persons not employed there visited the premises."

During his time in Taunton, Correiro stayed at a boarding house on Lane Avenue, near the brick company. Correiro appeared to want to be left alone but showed no behavior that raised anyone's suspicions. He seemed to have no money, and no watch had been displayed.

As June 15th drew near, rumors began that the Correiro preliminary hearing would be postponed. The Borden trial was not yet over and seemed as though it would not be so at any time soon. (In fact, it would not end until June 20th.)

On June 13, Joseph M. Chaves of Fall River wrote a letter to the editors of the *Daily Herald*, which the newspaper reprinted in full. Chaves wanted to know why Jose Correiro had been treated so differently from Lizzie Borden, even though both had been accused of the same level of crime. For example, stated Chaves, visitors had been denied access to speak with him, whereas Lizzie Borden could receive visitors daily. (The writer claimed the police would grant access to Correiro, but only if the conversation was in English, which, of course, Correiro could not understand.)

Captain Philip Harrington, having read the article, protested. He stated that visitation with Correiro was limited because it was not "right to allow everybody, who wishes to gratify a morbid curiosity, to enter the cell corridor just for the sake of glaring through the bars at the prisoner." Anyone with direct interest in the case was allowed entry, however.

The efforts of the Portuguese community spread beyond Fall River. On the morning of June 14, Portuguese Consul Viscount de Valle da Costa of Boston arrived in Fall River. (His birth name was Manoel P.F. d'Almeida.) The *Fall River Daily Globe* reported that da Costa visited Portuguese community leader Joseph M. Chaves. The *Boston Globe* wrote that the viscount "had engaged first-class talent." The *Daily Herald* reported that da Costa spent the better part of the day at the Ferry Street train terminal waiting for the Boston attorney but said counsel did not arrive.

At 4 o'clock, Chaves, da Costa, and Rev. Augustin Percot of St. Anne's Church, visited Correiro. As the Boston lawyer had not arrived, Marcus G.B. Swift (of Swift and Grime) was hired to represent Correiro and accompanied the other three.

June 15, 1893

The date for the preliminary hearing had now arrived. At 9 o'clock, Correiro and two other prisoners were escorted into the courtroom. Correiro's case was the first heard:

> During his confinement, he has undergone no physical change that was apparent and his imprisonment in the station cell has had but little effect upon him. He was attired in a new suit of clothes and presented a neater appearance than when first seen. He seemed to be cool and blissfully ignorant of what was transpiring. His restless eyes roved about the room taking in every object, and he evidently was particularly interested in the HERALD sketch artist whom he gave the benefit of long inquiring glances. (*FRDH*, June 15, 1893)

The Coolidges soon entered, followed in short order by Stephen and Freddie Manchester.

Lawyer Swift immediately asked for a further continuance, saying he had just been appointed as counsel and the defense needed time to prepare its case. During Swift's request, Consul da Costa entered the room. McDonough granted a continuance until June 22, one week hence:

> Dr. Dutra, acting as interpreter, imparted the information to Correiro who, at first, was unable to understand, but when it was explained he seemed satisfied and returned to his seat in the dock. A few minutes later, he was conducted to the cell room, where he was visited by the consul. The latter's presence assures the friends of Correiro that the prisoner will be justly dealt with. (*FRDH*, June 15, 1893)

As to the presence in Fall River of da Costa:

> Some of [Correiro's] friends considered that he was being unjustly treated and it was on account of this report that the consul at Boston was communicated with.
>
> The latter received instructions from his government, in answer to his inquiry, to see that Correiro received fair treatment. The consul immediately engaged the services of Judge Hutchinson, a Boston lawyer of repute, and came to this city Wednesday. A slight sickness prevented Mr. Hutchinson from coming and M.G.B. Swift Esq., was consulted. (*FRDH*, June 15, 1893)

Viscount da Costa left for New York City immediately after court was adjourned.

The witness list was released to the press. It included:

Stephen Manchester	Jennie F. Coolidge	John Tonsall
Frederick Manchester	W. W. Coolidge	Joseph Lacroix
Eli Brissette	Manuel Souci	Albion C. Cook
Edward Leduc	Mathias Mosher	Robert G. Blake
James Monaghan	Albert Deane	Joseph Duarte
John Pedao	Mrs. John Pedao	Thomas King
John Coughlin	Hiram Brightman	Dr. William A. Dolan
Dr. George S. Eddy	Dr. Dwight E. Cone	Dr. Herbert G. Wilbur

(Some of the above names varied in spelling according to the source.) The *Fall River Daily Globe* reported that all were placed under $200 appearance bonds. However, it is more likely that only those whose appearance was questionable would have been so treated.

June 16 – June 21, 1893

Since Correiro's arrest, the police had assured the press and, by extension, the public that they had their man in the murder case. For whatever reason, upon the further continuance of the case, the police released the most damning information so far. About ten days earlier, Correiro had confessed. Upon doing so, he told the police where he had hidden the watch and pocketbook.

The night he made his confession, Marshal Hilliard and Captains Desmond, Doherty, and Connors drove to the place. They searched until nearly morning and returned without the watch:

> The next night the same person [persons?] with the prisoner and his Honor, the Mayor, and a carriage driver from Stone's stable went to the scene.
>
> Correiro was handcuffed to Captain Desmond, the right hand being shackled. He directed the party to the location; got down on his knees and with his left hand delved into the earth and drew forth the watch and the pocketbook. He then passed the articles into his right hand.
>
> With this member chained to Captain Desmond he passed the evidence of his guilt to his Honor the Mayor and at the same time raised his hat with the left hand.
>
> City Marshal Hilliard was an interested spectator. That was all Mr. Hilliard was allowed to do. This finding of the watch was looked upon as a secret of the department, which must be kept and it was known only to the men who were present.
>
> Mayor Coughlin was vehement in his expression of a desire to keep the matter from the papers and threatened any officer with dismissal who should divulge it. It was not divulged by any policeman on the force. Every man held his tongue but the story was not told in its entirety until today the GLOBE gives the unvarnished facts. (*FRDG*, June 16, 1893)

The *Daily Herald* went further. It claimed that on June 6, one of its reporters strayed into the central police station about midnight. Just before midnight, a carriage had parked at the side door and out of it emerged Captains Connors, Desmond, and Doherty. Handcuffed to Doherty's left wrist was Correiro. The police, as described above, wished to keep all this from the press, but realized the reporter had seen them. An appeal was made to the *Daily Herald* to keep this information from print, and the newspaper honored the request.

In the meantime, the reporter, now aware of the case regarding Correiro, continued to investigate the situation and approached the police with the facts he had unearthed. Because the police realized they could no longer answer "We don't know," they gave the reporter the full story.

On the night the reporter saw the incident at the police station, the captains had been guided by Correiro "to the Highland road." At a point about three-quarters of a mile from the Manchester farm, Correiro led the policemen to a stone wall and pulled from it the watch. (We see this differs somewhat from the *Daily Globe* report.)

According to the reporter, Correiro admitted killing Bertha, but had no preconceived plan to do so. He had entered the house only to steal things:

> He found no one at home. He then went into the bedroom and had already taken the watch and pocketbook, when Bertha surprised him. She commanded him to put the things down, and he refused. She seized the axe and he struck her in the mouth with his fist. There was a scuffle for the possession of the weapon. He got it and killed her.
>
> He then went and tossed the axe into the woodpile and passed through the orchard. When 400 yards west of the house and the same distance south of the Wilson road, he stopped in the woods near three large stones and buried the watch and the bloody pocketbook. (*FRDG*, June 17, 1893)

We see here that the *Daily Globe* report contradicts the statements by Joseph Lacroix and Manuel Sousa that Correiro took the coins he proffered out of a woman's pocketbook. It would seem likely that the newspaper was in error regarding their claim of the pocketbook being found with the watch since, at the time of the shoe purchase, Lacroix and Sousa knew nothing of the murder, let alone that a pocketbook was missing from the Manchester house. Thus, the two had no reason to mention a pocketbook unless they observed Correiro with it. (Of course, it could also be that Correiro took two pocketbooks from the house.)

Within a few days of Correiro's arrest, rumors had spread that he had confessed to the crime. The newspapers reported these rumors, saying police were not admitting to any such confession. Now that it was revealed that Correiro took the police to look for the watch on June 6, just a day after his arrest, the newspapers all touted with some glee that they had been right all along.

The papers now began widening their search for background information. Consul da Costa claimed he had visited Fall River to see that justice was being served regarding Correiro. He made no statement nor voiced an opinion of the Portuguese's guilt or innocence. However, on June 19th, da Costa returned to Fall River to speak with Correiro. The following day, the three Fall River dailies and the *Boston Globe* printed identical articles regarding da Costa's visit with Correiro. Given that da Costa's words were in quotation marks indicates that he issued a printed statement to the publications.

Da Costa reported that Correiro was born on the Azorean island of St. Michael and his only relatives in America were two cousins. At eighteen years old, Correiro was considered a minor, and da Costa felt it his duty to visit him. The consul arrived in the city feeling Correiro was innocent, unless the prisoner told him otherwise.

Correiro did tell him. The consul related to the reporters that after Correiro's last employment with Manchester, the Portuguese spent several days with Muniz. Correiro had no money and, after a few days, Muniz told him he could no longer stay at his house. The destitute Correiro left, owning only the clothes on his back. These included a badly worn pair of shoes that were full of holes.

Upon leaving the Manchester farm, Correiro felt he was still owed money. Manchester refused to pay. It was Correiro's belief that Manchester kept money in his house. Therefore, in his dire straits, Correiro felt he would be justified in going to the farm and taking the money he was owed.

The consul now told of the encounter at the Manchester house, a story that made more sense than the ones previously in the newspapers. According to da Costa, Correiro was turned out of the Muniz house the day before the murders, not the morning of the murders as had been previously reported. Therefore, all the awkward timelines in getting Correiro to the Manchester farm on Memorial Day morning that had been proposed were not necessary. Rather, Correiro merely hid near the farm early Memorial Day morning until Manchester left on his milk route. (Of course, this indicates a criminal intention, as Correiro could have again approached Manchester directly, but did not do so.) Correiro then entered the kitchen. Bertha was there and he told her he wanted the money owed to him. Some argument occurred, during which Bertha seized the axe from the woodbox. He refused to leave and she came at him with the axe. The slight Portuguese felt the strong young woman could overpower him and somehow wrestled the axe from her and struck her. The attack on Bertha was not premeditated; Correiro brought no weapon with him.

The consul told reporters that in the last fifty years only one previous homicide was committed by a Portuguese. He deplored Correiro's actions for their reflection on his country.

The story given by da Costa is notable in two ways. First, da Costa claims Correiro *did not* leave the Muniz house on the morning of Memorial Day, as Muniz claimed but, rather, left the day before. Until this point, any analysis of the case afforded Correiro at least some degree of possible innocence in that he had to cover long distances on foot within a very constricted timeline. But, now we see that Correiro had the opportunity to be at the farm very early Memorial Day morning. Bertha was probably killed between seven and eight o'clock. This also gave time for Correiro to buy the shoes and travel to Crab Pond bridge to see Stephen Manchester at 11 o'clock.

Secondly, the story told by da Costa makes sense in every detail. That destitution would cause Correiro to go to the Manchester farm is believable. The new information, showing that the Portuguese could be at the farm early in the morning, avoids the previous timing questions. That Correiro was unarmed, assuming this was true, shows he did not anticipate violence, and that he wanted only money indicates why no sexual attack was made.

It is unclear, however, as to why da Costa would tell all this to the press. It might be construed that Correiro's taking the police to the hiding place of the watch was a form of confession, but clearly no formal document had been so filed. Correiro, to this point, had pleaded not guilty. His preliminary hearing was yet a few days away. It is a mystery why da Costa did not wait until after that trial to tell his incriminating story.

On the morning of June 21, Stephen Manchester, while on his delivery route, stopped a reporter from the *Fall River Daily Globe*. Manchester had not seen the da Costa article, but asked the reporter about a previous report in the newspaper that Correiro had confessed. The reporter said he had, and then told Manchester about the da Costa story.

Manchester was incensed that he had been accused of not paying Correiro some of his wages. "I paid every cent [to Correiro] before he left," said Manchester, referring to Correiro's doing the agreed-upon work and wages. "I owe no man anything and if you will go around and inquire you will find that I have as good a home in this respect as one could wish." Manchester refused to believe Bertha had the axe first. Rather, he thought Correiro went to the farm for immoral intentions toward Bertha. Manchester made this statement based on his belief that Correiro so approached Bertha and, when she rebuffed him, he grabbed the axe and attacked her. Manchester expressed the desire to have a go with Correiro with the axe.

A reporter for the *Daily Evening News* also came across Manchester, who told him the same story as above. However, he added that when he and his son saw Correiro at Crab Pond bridge, Freddie pointed out Correiro's new shoes.

CHAPTER 7
THE PRELIMINARY HEARING

June 22, 1893

There were now no more delays. At 9:45 a.m. on Thursday, June 22, the preliminary hearing of Jose Correiro began before Judge John J. McDonough.

The court's docket was not limited to just this one celebrated case. As had happened at the preliminary hearing for Lizzie Borden, many hearings were scheduled:

> While the other cases were being tried the numerous witnesses and interested parties were arriving, and just before the case was called M.G.B. Swift entered the court room, accompanied by Consul De Costa and Judge P. Henry Hutchinson. Lawyer J.L. DeTerra [J.I. da Terra] of New Bedford, who has been associated with the case, was also present.
>
> Stephen C. Manchester and his sisters, together with Freddie Manchester and Mr. and Mrs. Coolidge, arrived early, and at 9 o'clock the prisoner, Correiro, was brought upstairs and placed in the same seat occupied by him at the time of his arraignment. He looked much better than on previous occasions and was attired in clothes of dark material. (*FRDH*, June 22, 1893)

When the Correiro case was called at about 10:00, the prisoner entered a plea of not guilty.

No stenographic report of the trial exists. However, the newspapers reported on the testimony in narrative fashion. (A reconstructed version of a transcript is provided in the Addendum.) The Borden trial had ended on June 20th so, in theory, Hosea Knowlton was available for the state, although it is questionable how prepared he could be. However, the newspaper accounts not only do not list him as prosecution counsel, they list no prosecution counsel whatsoever. According to the *Fall River Daily*

Herald, Judge McDonough questioned the witnesses. Correiro's defense counsel then cross-examined them.

By all appearances, Marshal Hilliard handled the prosecution's case other than the questioning of the witnesses. According to the *Daily Herald*, Hilliard, "called upon 11 witnesses for the government." In the previous chapter, twenty-four possible witnesses were on the list. It is unclear if the smaller number here meant that Hilliard culled the list or that the remaining witnesses were for the defense.

At the Borden preliminary hearing, the medical examiner, Dr. William A. Dolan, was called first. Except for a brief interruption by the testimony of engineer Thomas Kieran providing measurements of the Borden house, Dolan's testimony comprised the entire first day of the hearing. Dolan remained on the stand the next morning. Dolan was still the medical examiner when Bertha Manchester was murdered, but the first witness called at this hearing was Bertha's father, Stephen.

As the father of the victim, and someone not suspected of involvement in the crime, it would be expected that Judge McDonough's questions were only of a background nature. Manchester was first asked to describe his movements on the morning of the murder. He did so, saying he left for his milk route about 7:30 in the morning. As he left the farm, he saw Bertha standing on the doorstep. It was the last time he saw her alive.

Manchester said he returned to the farm between 2:30 and 2:45 that afternoon. As he stopped the wagon at the barn door, his son Freddie got off the wagon and went to the house to get something to eat. Stephen and his hired boy, John Tonsall, went into the barn to unhitch the horse. Almost immediately, Freddie came running into the barn, yelling that Bertha had been killed. Manchester ran to the kitchen of the house and saw his daughter lying in a pool of blood. He could tell she had been dead for some time. (Thus, despite some newspapers having reported to the contrary, Manchester *had* gone directly to the house upon Freddie's awful revelation.)

McDonough asked Manchester if he recognized Correiro. Manchester said he did; the man had worked for him for two days, the last of which was about two weeks before the murder.

Marshal Hilliard produced the watch and McDonough asked Manchester if he recognized it. He said it had belonged to Bertha. Both it and her pocketbook had been taken by the murderer. (The pocketbook was not in evidence.)

Judge McDonough asked Manchester only about twenty questions. Now, on cross-examination, defense lawyer Swift had many more.

Swift asked for more detail as to the employment of Correiro. Manchester said Correiro first came to his farm at about five o'clock on October 31 or November 1 of 1892. He asked, "Job for me?" Manchester asked Correiro if he knew how to milk a cow. Correiro said he did, so Manchester replied, "I'll try you, then."

24. Stephen Manchester at the Preliminary Hearing. From the *Fall River Daily Herald*, June 22, 1893.

Correiro worked for Manchester the rest of that day. Then, Correiro ate supper and went to bed. The next morning, he did some chores. He ate breakfast but, for some unknown reason, then left the farm at about 6 o'clock. He did not return. Correiro then showed up at the farm in the middle of the following May, shortly before the murder.

Manchester decided to hire Correiro again. Manchester did not like the fact that Correiro did not speak English, since he had to be shown his tasks via hand signals. But Manchester observed that Correiro was a very good milker, which was obviously an important skill on a dairy farm. Again, Correiro worked the rest of that day. The next morning he accompanied Manchester on the milk delivery route through Fall River. Again, Correiro spent the night. He accompanied Manchester again on the milk route the following morning. About halfway through the deliveries, Correiro noticed two Portuguese on the sidewalk. After Correiro spoke to them, one of the Portuguese approached Manchester. Manchester had agreed to pay Correiro $15 a month, plus board. The Portuguese said Correiro would not stay for less than $20. Manchester refused to pay the higher amount, and Correiro did not return to the milk route.

Two days later, Correiro showed up at the farm around 3:30. He had left some possessions there and had come back to get them. Manchester paid him one dollar for the two days of work Correiro had done.

On an undisclosed day after that, Manchester ran into Correiro while on the milk route. Stephen's son Freddie urged his father to hire Correiro again. Two Portuguese happened by. Manchester told them he would pay $15 and board if Correiro wanted to come back. They told Correiro this and he agreed. Correiro got on the milk wagon and returned to the Manchester farm. He did some work and stayed overnight, but the next morning he left after breakfast.

Manchester did not see Correiro again until the day of the murder. Manchester was on his milk route. At about 11 o'clock, he was on Crab Pond bridge going south; Correiro, walking by in the opposite direction, turned his head and grinned. The two did not speak to each other. Manchester did not see Correiro again until the two were in the courtroom together at the first gathering for the preliminary hearing, a week before the present one.

Swift asked Manchester if he went directly home on the day of the murder after he finished his milk route. Manchester said he did not. He first stopped at his sisters' house. (Mary and Lucannah Manchester lived at 128 South Main Street.) After that, he proceeded down Main Street to the corner of Borden Street, where he bought some flowers for Bertha. He also stopped at Joe Cadieux's store (at 276 Pleasant Street) to purchase some grain. He did not look at his watch, but thought it was about 2:30 when he got home.

His son Freddie and a hired boy, John Tonsall, were with him on the milk route. Previous to Tonsall, Manchester said he had had "a Frenchman" working for him, but the man had since left his employ.

Swift asked Manchester for more details of his actions once finding out that Bertha had been murdered. After coming into the kitchen, Manchester said, he looked at her body, but did not touch her. He saw a wound over her mouth and another on her forehead, but the serious wounds were on the back of her skull. After quickly going through the rooms, he harnessed his horse and drove as fast as he could to tell the marshal about the crime.

Swift then asked several seemingly trivial questions. How old was Bertha? (Twenty-two.) Did she graduate from high school? (No.) How many cows did he keep? (Nineteen.) How many acres did he own? (Forty.)

How many barns did he have? (Two, but one was used only for storage.)

Swift asked Stephen if he kept an axe in the house. Manchester said he did; it was kept in or next to the woodbox. He had seen the axe, covered with blood, in the possession of the police after the murder.

Stephen testified that the "Frenchman" he had employed had left the farm about two weeks before the murders.

Stephen said that Bertha kept the house and fed the chickens and horses.

Getting back to information pertinent to the case, Swift asked Manchester about Bertha's possessions. He said she had a watch, the trade dollar, the half-dollar with the hole in it, some rings and other trinkets, and a little boy's watch. However, Manchester could not remember the last time he saw any of these.

Manchester said that he did not know the name of the officer he saw at the police station. Leaving there, he went to his sisters' house on South Main Street. One of them got in the wagon with him (he did not say whether it was Mary or Lucannah). They then drove to his daughter Jennie's house. She also boarded the wagon. The three drove to the farm; Manchester found Dr. Dolan and the police were already there.

Swift moved on to the watch in evidence. Manchester said he had purchased it about two-and-a-half years earlier from Foster's (pawnbroker J.A. Foster & Co.) on Pleasant Street. The case had been engraved with the initials B.M.M. by J.H. Franklin & Co. It was then confirmed that these initials were on the watch in evidence. Marshal Hilliard then presented to the court the receipt for the watch, which had the serial number 2,377,280.

Stephen Manchester then left the stand. He had testified for a little more than an hour.

Next called was F.M. Chase, who said he was a jeweler. He confirmed that the serial number on the watch matched his records of being sold to Stephen Manchester.

Bristol County Medical Examiner Dr. William A. Dolan was now called. He had just begun testifying about his actions on the morning of May 30 when the defense counsel asked for a moment to confer. The court granted a five-minute recess. Upon the court reconvening, attorney Swift, speaking for Correiro, said he "thought it proper and suitable to waive further examination in this matter as far as the court is concerned."

With this stunning comment, Judge McDonough found Correiro "probably guilty." The prisoner was committed without bail to the Taunton jail, to await the finding of the grand jury in the superior court to be held in November.

At 1:29 that afternoon, Correiro was on the train for Taunton, escorted by Officers Adelard Perron and George Allen. At the jail there, just as had been the case with Lizzie Borden, he would spend the months waiting for the grand jury's findings to indict him for the death of Bertha Manchester. The newspapers anticipated the charge to the grand jury would be for manslaughter. If tried and convicted of this crime, the maximum sentence would be twenty years. Given the horrific nature of the murder, it would seem likely Correiro would get the maximum.

CHAPTER 8
THE WHEELS OF JUSTICE

Given all the evidence against him, the *Boston Globe* questioned why Correiro's counsel decided to have Stephen Manchester testify at the preliminary hearing instead of just waiving examination. Certainly, there was nothing Attorney Swift could have presented that would have freed his client.

In an interview, the lawyer told the newspaper that his intention was to lessen the charge. Manchester testified that Bertha was well-built and feisty. She was the kind who would likely put up a fight if challenged. This would bolster the argument that Jose had not gone there with evil intent, but that the violence erupted due to an argument spinning out of control.

Swift laid out how he would present his case at trial. He would argue that Correiro did not strike Bertha in the face with his fist; that is, he was not threatening or attacking her. Rather, the axe was seized by Bertha and, in the struggle for it, the weapon hit her face, knocking out two teeth.

Swift said Correiro would take the stand to tell his story. He would claim that he went to the house only to seek work. Finding no one in the house, his destitute condition led to the impulse to search the house for valuables. He ransacked two rooms but, before he could exit the house, Bertha came into the kitchen and found him in the dining room. Bertha seized the axe from the wood box and a struggle ensued. "Mad passion" came over him and, once able to wrest the axe from Bertha, he repeatedly hit her in the head with it until she was dead.

Now panicking, Correiro ran out of the house and threw the axe down. He ran to the rear of the property, through the orchard, and eventually found a spot to hide the watch and pocketbook. He then proceeded to Wilson Road, where a farmer saw him. He walked to Bowenville, as had been described in other reports.

Swift told the reporter that Correiro did not sleep in the woods the night before the murder but left for New Boston Road after eating breakfast at a friend's house.

Although the Court had ordered Correiro held until the action of the Bristol County Grand Jury in November, it so happened that a session was in progress in New Bedford. Although no change to the legal decree was evident, in late June, just a week after the preliminary hearing, the Fall River newspapers reported that an attempt would be made to present the Correiro case at the sitting session. As the session ended on June 30th, things had to happen fast. The *Daily News* said the case would be presented on the 28th; the *Fall River Daily Globe* said June 29th was the more likely date. The *Daily News* appeared to be surer of its sources, claiming Marshal Hilliard, Captains Desmond, Doherty, Connors, Steven Manchester, and one or two other witnesses had been summoned.

The *Daily News* stated, "the probabilities are that an indictment for murder in the second degree will be found, as the police are not now inclined to believe that there was premeditation or malice aforethought" (June 28, 1893). The *Daily Globe* agreed that there was some question as to what the charge would be, saying, "there are those who believe that the State cannot make out a clear case of murder against the accused" (June 28, 1893).

The *Daily Herald* reported that "the friends and relatives of Joseph Correiro were at the city hall again today endeavoring to do something to insure the prolonging of the prisoner's life." The group proposed to hire "able lawyers" for their countryman, although there is no indication as to why his current ones were deficient. Further, said the paper, the Portuguese "are seeking the sympathy of most of the influential persons in the community." In doing so, "they hope to arouse the same sympathy for their friend that swelled out so munificently for Lizzie Borden, and while they do not deny that he killed Bertha they anticipate open declarations of charity and mercy on the part of the authorities" (June 28, 1893).

As it happened, the newspapers were correct about the sitting grand jury hearing the Correiro case. But they were incorrect as to the charge:

> The grand jury at New Bedford yesterday returned an indictment against Jose Correiro for the murder in the first degree in killing Bertha M. Manchester on May 30, Memorial day. This is a safe indictment for the government, under it a conviction can be brought for murder in the first degree, murder in the second degree or for manslaughter. Had the indictment been returned for murder in the second degree and the full evidence been sufficient to convict for murder in the first degree, the government would be debarred from taking advantage of it, as they could only ask for a verdict on a charge in the second degree. Under the indictment returned a verdict on any degree of homicide warranted by the evidence can be demanded.

> Correiro was not arraigned, and will probably be brought down from Taunton for his arraignment some time during the July sitting of the regular criminal term. (*FRDEN*, July 1, 1893)

The *Daily Herald* predicted that the trial would take place no later than September.

At the July 17 session of the superior court, Chief Justice Albert Mason consented to District Attorney Hosea Knowlton's request that decreed that Jose Correiro be arraigned at 9:00 on Wednesday, July 19. As was in the case of the preliminary hearing, M.G.B. Swift would represent Correiro.

In the Borden case, the *Fall River Daily Globe* had been the only local newspaper to indicate their belief that Lizzie Borden was guilty. The *Daily Evening News* and the *Daily Herald* were quick to point out rushes to judgment and what they considered exculpatory factors, such as Lizzie's social and church work. Now, in what might seem a bit of irony, those two newspapers seemed convinced Correiro would be convicted of the murders. It was only the *Daily Globe* who proposed an obstacle. In an article appearing one day before Correiro's arraignment, they brought up the issue of Correiro's confession:

> There is no doubt that Correiro was frightened into a confession, and he probably was not acquainted with his rights. He had no counsel. When he was arrested, the only thing that pointed to him as the guilty party, was a speck of blood on his shirt. He had purchased a new pair of shoes, to be sure, but he had a right to purchase them, and there was nothing to prove conclusively that the coins which he exchanged for the shoes, belonged to the victim. Nevertheless, he was arrested, and in a helpless condition was plied with questions and cross questions until he surrendered.
>
> Had he remained silent, he could not have been convicted and if the court treats him as though he had remained silent, it may be difficult to persuade 12 men that he committed the deed. However, that is not the point after all, because the court will not so treat him. The point is this: How does it happen that the authorities can seize an ignorant, penniless foreigner, organize a private inquest, torture him for hours, turn him and twist him and then use his admissions against him, while nobody in the length and breadth of the land protests?
>
> That is the question which a good many people are asking. Not people of influence, perhaps, but people who can think and do think, and who draw comparisons. The regularly organized inquest is a mild ordeal compared to star chamber proceedings, in which Correiro has figured. From the first, the police assumed that he was guilty, and while they held a few suspects, they bent all their energies to the capture of the Portuguese.

> Once they had him in their toils, they compelled him to incriminate himself. It has been agreed with the claim, that a person who is practically under arrest, (which means a person who is not arrested, but who may be arrested, if circumstances warrant it) cannot be handicapped by anything he may say, to those who examine him in an attempt to extract the truth from him. Correiro was not only practically under arrest, but he was in durance vile [imprisoned], and it is singular enough that such a dissection as that to which he was subjected is tolerated.
>
> Had Correiro been warned by a lawyer to keep his lips sealed, the grand jury might have indicted him, but he would have gone free. He was seen by the father of the murdered girl on the morning of the tragedy, and the mere fact that he, or somebody who resembles him, was observed on the Wilson Road on Memorial Day, does not connect him with the crime. Mr. Manchester can not identify the coins in Correiro's possession, and the burden is on the State to show where he secured them. Inasmuch as the law is said to be no respecter of persons, the trial of the Portuguese will be well worth studying. (July 18, 1893)

The newspaper's statement, that "it has been agreed with the claim, that a person who is practically under arrest. . . cannot be handicapped by anything he may say, to those who examine him in an attempt to extract the truth from him," is an obvious reference to the Borden case. In his opinion as to the admissibility of Lizzie Borden's inquest testimony, Justice Mason stated:

> The common law regards substance more than form. The principle involved cannot be evaded by avoiding the form of arrest if the witness at the time of such testimony is practically in custody. From the agreed facts and the facts otherwise in evidence, it is plain that the prisoner at the time of her testimony was, so far as relates to this question, as effectually in custody as if the formal precept had been served; and, without dwelling on other circumstances which distinguish the facts of this case from those of cases on which the Government relies, we are all of opinion that this consideration is decisive, and the evidence is excluded. (*Trial*, 830–831)

With those words, Mason sustained lawyer George Robinson's motion to disallow Lizzie Borden's inquest testimony.

Given that Judge McDonough had decreed on June 22 that Correiro's case would be presented to the grand jury in November, his counsel obviously assumed that any trial would be at least six months away. Now, however, instead of an indictment taking more than four months, it had taken only one week, and Correiro's arraignment in the Superior Court would be less than three weeks after that.

There are no records regarding lawyer Swift's knowledge of this shortened timeline. However, while indications are that the police and prosecution had had their way so far, it was now time for Swift to throw a wrench into the gears.

Court was called into session on the morning of July 19 and, as had been so ordered by Justice Mason two days earlier, Jose Correiro was seated in the courtroom:

> Correiro, as he sat in the dock, presented the appearance of a sallow-faced youth. His face was rather long, cheek bones were prominent; nose thin and quite large black or dark eyes, quite deeply sunken; a protruding forehead; small black mustache and black hair growing low down on the forehead.
>
> It was not the face of a hardened prisoner, there was nothing sinister about the countenance. That he is of a nervous temperament was evidenced by the twitching of the muscles of the face as he sat for several hours in the court prior to his arraignment. (*FRDG*, July 19, 1893)

His appearance was strikingly different from that he displayed around Fall River that spring:

> Correiro was dressed in a dark brown or black coat, vest and pantaloons, and a cream colored outing shirt, and by his side on a settee rested a soft slouch hat of dark blue or black. (*FRDG*, July 19, 1893)

In addition to Attorney Swift, Portuguese Consul Viscount de Valle da Costa was present, telling the newspapers that, once again, his attendance was only to assure that the rights of his countryman were preserved. Lawyer J. I. da Terra of New Bedford also was present.

Swift told the court that the defendant was not yet prepared to make a plea and requested it be postponed. This was not granted outright, but Justice Mason gave the prosecution and defense two hours to work things out. Correiro's three representatives, along with District Attorney Knowlton, left for Knowlton's office down the street from the courthouse, while the Court proceeded with other cases.

The group returned to the courthouse at 10:30. Upon the case being called, it was time for Swift to present his bombshell to the Court: His client could not be charged with this crime. The grand jury had indicted Jose Correiro for the murder of Bertha M. Manchester. But the man sitting here was not Jose Correiro; his name was Jose Correa de Mello, a man who had been charged with nothing. In conjunction with this, Swift filed a formal plea of misnomer with the Court. (The plea is reproduced in the Addendum.)

No such claim was made by Swift, or anyone else, until that morning, said Knowlton. But while the plea may seem quite serious, Knowlton was non plussed:

> Just before court adjourned, the district attorney arose and read the above plea. He said that although the name under which he was indicted was given by Mr. Swift and had been tried in the lower court under it, yet in a case of that sort he didn't desire to make an issue, as it was of trivial consequence.

However, Knowlton pointed out to the court that it would be some time before a scheduled session of the grand jury would be held:

> He suggested a special session be called for at an early date, for next week if possible. Chief Justice Mason ordered that the grand jury be called in for a special session Monday next, and the court took a recess.
>
> The indictment which will be reported at the special session will read just as the other did except that the name Jose Correa de Mello will be substituted for Jose Correiro. (*FRDEN*, July 19, 1893)

It must be here noted that the accused in the case has always here been referred to as Jose Correiro. This was done deliberately. Until Swift's plea, Correiro was the name that was always used in legal or newspaper accounts—reasonable, since there was no indication that this was not his real name. Also, consider that after Bertha Manchester's murder, the police had no solid leads. While they thought it quite possible that Bertha was killed by a former farm worker, and likely a Portuguese, the group of choice for the police when a crime was committed in Fall River at that time, they had no identifiable person in mind. Stephen Manchester called his last Portuguese worker Manuel; he did not even know the worker's real name. Through investigation, the police settled on Correiro, whose name was given to them by someone in the Portuguese community. There is no indication that the informants or any other Portuguese the police interviewed thought that the suspect's name was anything but Correiro. If I, as author, at the outset had used the name de Mello, while ever reference used different names, it would be awkward and confusing.

The question now becomes how his name should be displayed henceforth. There is no simple answer. When he was "Correiro," his surname was spelled multiple ways in various newspaper accounts. At times the name was spelled two different ways in the same article. The same was true with his "new" name after the plea of misnomer.

This phenomenon is due partly to the sloppiness of the news industry at the time. Apparently little effort was spent on confirming the spelling of names or places. Even legal records at that time were inconsistent. This inconsistency was magnified in this case because the accused had a foreign name. Further, it should be noted that Portuguese names are complex. They often do not follow hard-and-fast rules. The prefixes "de" and "da" translate to "of." However, such prefix is not considered essential. Therefore, the prisoner's name could be written Jose de Mello or Jose Mello.

Each of the three Fall River daily newspapers printed the plea of misnomer. The *Daily Globe* and *Daily Herald* used "De Mello." The *Daily Evening News* used "de Mello." The *Boston Globe* also printed the plea, using the spelling "de Mello." Thus, the newspapers do not agree, even though each was supposedly reprinting the same document.

Henceforth, the name "de Mello" will be used. This is done for two reasons. First, the four newspapers agree that there is a space between de/ De and Mello. It is further noted that two other Portuguese involved with the case, de Terra and da Costa are shown with a similar space. Secondly, the big-city *Boston Globe* was the highest-ranking newspaper of those quoted, so their representation of the plea of misnomer is the most likely to be correct.

Unfortunately, there is no such consistent form from this point forward in the newspapers insofar as his name. Some call him Correa, some Correa de Mello, some de Mello and others Mello. The *Boston Globe* stuck with the name Correiro even after Attorney Swift's plea of misnomer was accepted. Therefore, the reader must recognize that any (or even alternative spellings) of the above refer to de Mello when the various versions are used in quoted references.

It would seem unlikely that Swift thought his ploy would do anything but buy time since, after all, he had had more than a month to advise the district attorney of any name change. But Swift may not have anticipated that Knowlton would ask for a special session of the grand jury or, even if so, that Mason would decree it.

The special grand jury session proceeded as dictated on the following Monday:

> The grand jury met in special session at New Bedford this forenoon and indicted Jose Correa de Mello, for the murder of Bertha May Manchester, on May 30.
>
> The jury was out about five minutes and returned an indictment similar to the old one in every respect except the name was changed from "Jose Correiro" to "Jose Correa de Mello." (*FRDG*, July 24, 1893)

Swift did gain additional time. The grand jury's action, although done with celerity, essentially started the legal processes again with a new indictment. De Mello's counsel had to be served the necessary papers and a new date scheduled for the arraignment.

When the Portuguese community announced its intention to find first-rate lawyers for their countryman, they probably assumed the grand jury would not hear the case until November, as that is what Judge McDonough had decreed at the preliminary hearing. Now, things had moved forward much faster. According to the *Daily Herald*, what the Portuguese now heard completely deflated the intended aggressive campaign:

> There has been a change of feeling among the countrymen of the accused murderer of Bertha Manchester. When Correiro or de Mello as he is now known, was first arrested the Portuguese of the city were strongly convinced of his innocence. Committees were selected to raise funds to engage counsel to defend him, and other committees were selected to assist in a general canvass among the Portuguese of the state in behalf of the man.
>
> The confession of the murderer led to a startling change. He was defended by his people because he was thought to be innocent, but when from his own lips an admission to the contrary was obtained, then the current of opinion veered. Up to that point large sums of money had been promised.
>
> When, however, it was found that De Mello was guilty of the terrible crime many withdrew from their agreement. They were willing, they said, to aid an innocent man, but not a guilty man, one self-condemned of so terrible a crime.
>
> Up to the present time not over $50 have been collected in this city, and there is no prospect of obtaining any more. Those who were at first most earnest in their work for the prisoner have relaxed their efforts and many of them have given up altogether.
>
> Throughout the country the collectors have given up their work. The lawyers' fees will have to come from other sources. A prominent Portuguese, in conversation with a HERALD man this morning, said his people had no desire, in fact they had absolutely refused, to assist De Mello when they knew that he had acknowledged his guilt. (*FRDH*, July 27, 1893)

All delays were exhausted on the morning of Monday, September 18. Jose Correa de Mello was arraigned before Superior Court Judge John Hopkins in Taunton. The defendant pleaded not guilty. He told the court he had no money and asked for counsel to be provided.

Consul Viscount de Valle da Costa was present and said he would aid in de Mello's defense. Judge Hopkins asked Correa if he had a preference for counsel. De Mello said he would like P.H. Hutchinson. The judge reserved decision. De Mello was then returned to jail.

CHAPTER 9
AUTUMN 1893

The de Mello case could not move forward until a lawyer was assigned and, subsequently, when a trial date was set. However, other events ancillary to the case transpired after the arraignment of de Mello.

JACINTHO MUNIZ MACHADO

On June 2, Fall River aldermen had authorized a $500 reward for information leading "to the discovery, apprehension and conviction of the person or persons who murdered Miss Bertha Manchester."

Only four days later, the *Daily Herald* questioned if the reward would be paid out:

> If it turns out that Correiro is the murderer of Miss Bertha Manchester, some question may arise regarding the reward which has been offered for the capture of the murderer, says the Providence Journal. In case the police who worked up the clue are barred, the prisoner's uncle may put in a claim which could be disputed, should it appear he brought his nephew under orders. There is a law which makes it necessary for any citizen who is called on to assist in an arrest and perhaps the money belongs to nobody. However, the city will take no pains to economize in this direction, provided the real villain is safe behind bars. (June 6, 1893)

Indeed, Jacintho Muniz Machado (aka Jacinto Muniz) did put in a claim for the reward. However, on the same day as de Mello's arraignment, the *Daily Herald* reported that the $500 reward might not be paid out to Machado or anyone else. As it happened, de Mello was arrested on June 4. Within the two-day interim, the mayor had not signed the authorization. As such, the city had decided to decline any payouts.

The strangest aspect of this is that it was Mayor Coughlin who had called the board to a special meeting where he read a prepared order asking that they authorize the reward. There was lament all around that by statute the maximum amount of the reward was limited to $500. The $500 reward was then approved unanimously by the aldermen.

We thus see that, on June 2, the aldermen authorized an order written by Coughlin himself. Therefore, there was no reason that Coughlin needed time to review the authorization—not only had he had written it, in fact, he was standing there when the board unanimously approved it. He could have signed it right away. Yet, he had not done so then, or even by two days later. At the risk of suggesting something perhaps less than honest was in play, the board's action meant the newspapers would announce the award to the public, yet Coughlin's not signing the order meant it would not be paid out should someone later try to claim it.

Things got much worse for Jacintho Muniz Machado that year. By all accounts, much of the Portuguese community had since turned against him, many of whom thought he cooperated with the police only for the purposes of claiming the reward money.

The *Fall River Daily Evening News* reported that Machado had received a letter from de Mello's family in the Azores, "wanting to know his reasons for having done what he did and directly accusing him of having received money for Jose's life" (Nov. 14, 1893). Upon receipt of the letter, Machado went to the Taunton jail to see his nephew. De Mello refused to see Machado, accusing his uncle of treachery and saying he was welcome to the reward.

There are reports that this rebuff weighed heavily on Machado. He soon became ill and, on November 14, only weeks after the letter from the Azores arrived, he died of typhoid pneumonia at his home in the Narragansett Mills block. He was only thirty-eight years old. Those still close to him said he never recovered from the events of the summer.

The *Fall River Daily Herald* reported that Frank Silvia, who had acted as an interpreter when de Mello was brought into the Fall River police station by Machado, had also received similar threats both from Fall River and the Azores.

Stephen and Mary Jane (Whittles) Manchester

While the loss of his daughter was certainly the worst thing that happened to Stephen Manchester in 1893, his life after the crime did not improve.

The divorce case had been continued in April. On October 16, the case was continued yet one more day, at the request of Stephen's lawyer. Finally, Superior Court case 479 and counter suit 492 were heard on October 17th at 2 p.m.

While the press had shown some interest in the case in January, Stephen Manchester was now not just a disgruntled husband but also a grieving father whose plight was well known by everyone in Fall River. The Whittles drownings (described in the chapter on the Manchesters) had occurred in 1890, before the January 1893 hearings, but now the sole family survivor, young Edwin, would testify on behalf of his aunt, Stephen's wife, Mary Jane.

The counsels for the two parties had not changed; Milton Reed appeared for Mary Jane and A. E. Bragg for Stephen. The *Daily Globe* reported:

> In her declaration she set up that she was always faithful and that he was cruel and abusive. For answer he said that she was always unfaithful and then she deserted him. (Oct. 18, 1893)

Stephen testified first. He thought the marriage took place in 1884, but did not know the date. (We see here that Stephen was probably in trouble long before the divorce hearings.) Mary Jane had left him several times. Again, he did not know the dates. Each time she came back of her own free will; he neither drove her away nor solicited her return.

Asked by his lawyer about the last time Mary Jane left him, Stephen recounted the incident with eighteen-month-old Alexander abusing the rooster. He did not see her for four years, but one day after that period she returned, with Alexander in tow, saying she had come back to go to work. By chance, Stephen had been quite ill at the time of her appearance, but he arose from the sofa and told her he had no use for her and would not have her in the house. "Bertha gave her five or six apples and she went out. As for being cruel to her, I never was, and I didn't hurt the child."

On cross-examination, Stephen said that, before their marriage, Mary Jane had not been his housekeeper but rather his domestic, although he did not describe the distinction. Asked how long she served in this capacity, not surprisingly, Stephen said he did not know. In her favor, he admitted she was a hard worker. Told that Mary Jane had been sick and poor during the four-year absence, Stephen said he had been unaware of this.

Lawyer Reed then asked Stephen about the crying incident. Stephen recounted it, saying the child kept up a "dismal howling until 12:30 and I could not sleep." He said, "I knocked on the partition and said: 'Mary in the name of God why don't you stop that child from crying. I want to sleep.'" In response, "She sassed me for that and got up, put on her clothes and left the house." Stephen had admitted he said he would throw the baby out of the window but did not actually touch the child. In fact, he did not leave his bedroom, and Mary Jane and Alexander were in the next room. When she left, she went to Charles Reed's house. (Charles Reed lived across New Boston Road. It is unclear if it was coincidence that her lawyer had the same surname or if there was some family connection.) The next exchange resulted in some courtroom levity:

> Reed - Could the child walk then?
>
> Witness [Manchester]- No, but it could yell. (*FRDG*, Oct. 18, 1893)

Although Manchester had requested custody of the child in his divorce petition, the following exchange indicates something less than a close family bond:

> Reed - Didn't you ask if the child had a good home [during Mary Jane's absence]?
>
> Witness [Manchester] - No, it didn't make any difference to me. She left a good home and it was her own fault. I always let her have her own way, and she could come or go as she liked. (*FRDG*, Oct. 18, 1893)

Pressed on how he acted when Mary Jane reappeared after a four-year absence, Manchester said:

> She dared me to strike her, and I think she wanted me to criminate myself so she could fix me. She wanted to go to work then, and said she could scrub any floor I had in 15 minutes, but I didn't want her. (*FRDG*, Oct. 18, 1893)

It then came to light that there was some wealth in the family. Stephen conceded he was one of the heirs of the estates of brothers Benjamin and Abraham:

> Mr. Reed - Would you take $75,000 for your share?
>
> Witness [Manchester] - I don't know that I would. I am not prepared to answer that question. (*FRDG*, Oct. 18, 1893)

He also said he owned land on Watuppa "lake," but "never saw it in my life."

Stephen's whaling life has been described earlier in the book. When asked when his father died, Stephen replied, "In 1876 when I was sailing around Cape Horn." This exchange, as reported by the *Daily Globe*, cannot be correct. It was shown that Stephen married his first wife in Fall River in 1864. It is clear from other records that he did not return to the sea after that.

Records indicate Stephen's father Benjamin died on January 10, 1864. We also saw that a man named Stephen Manchester was reported as being on the whaling ship *Tamerlane*, which left port in 1862 and returned in 1865, but it was shown that this was not true, due to Stephen's then having to be in two places at the same time. Why he said his father died in 1876 is a mystery, although it might have been an error on the part of the reporter. In any event, Manchester claimed he was at sea at this time.

Stephen's older daughter, Jennie Coolidge, now testified. She said she had graduated from high school. (Interestingly, farm-daughter Jennie graduated, but upper-scale Lizzie Borden did not.) She was still at home at the time her father married Mary Jane Whittles. She eventually became a schoolteacher and, at that time, Bertha was going to high school. Bertha had to drop out of school to help run the farm. Of course, Bertha was not available to testify, but Jennie was allowed to repeat what Bertha had told her. Bertha was in the house and confirmed to Jennie that the baby was crying as her father described. She told Jennie that Stephen did threaten to throw the baby out of the window if the mother could not hush him up.

Jennie said she was present when her stepmother scolded her father, but never saw the two come to blows. She agreed with her father about Mary Jane's work ethic and being an unfaithful wife.

In testimony befitting Emma or Lizzie Borden, Jennie said she had no complaint about Mary Jane's treatment of her, but that Mary Jane never filled the place of a mother. When asked about stepbrother Alexander, Jennie said she would not know him if she met him on the street. She added:

> I did not interest myself in the boy, nor did any of the other members of my family, to my knowledge. (*FRDEN*, Oct. 18, 1893)

Heretofore, only from Stephen had been heard from regarding the rooster incident, but now Thomas McDonald testified. He had worked for Stephen at the time. He did not see Alexander assault the rooster but arrived at the scene in time to see Stephen "swipe the kid with a bludgeon, or something." He went on to say he did not know "whether it was a club, the butt end of a whip stick, the limb of a tree or a stick." The shrieks of the child caused Mary Jane to exit the house in a rage. McDonald said he boarded at the farm for two months (which sounds like a record span for an employee of Stephen Manchester) and this was the only unusual exchange he ever saw between the husband and wife.

The next witness was Stephen's sister, Nancy Downing. She said that, by coincidence, she had heard Stephen was sick and made her way to his farm. Another woman got off the horse car at the same time she did, and both women started walking up Wilson Road toward the Manchester farm. The women conversed and Nancy discovered she was speaking to Stephen's second wife, although she did not say where she was going. Apparently, Nancy Downing walked faster and arrived first at the farm. She found Stephen to be quite ill and lying on the lounge. She told Stephen about the encounter and advised him it was likely Mary Jane would be arriving soon. Nancy confirmed the exchange between Stephen and Mary Jane. She, too, entered the fray, begging Mary Jane to leave the house and stop taunting her brother:

> Mr. Reed - What right had you to beg this woman to leave her own house?
>
> Witness [Nancy Downing] - Because Stephen was sick and she was annoying him. I wanted her to go away and come back when he was better. She went to sit down and I moved the chair away, but she didn't fall. She said, "How dare you take a chair from under me in my own house?" She staied [sic] until she got ready to go and then went out. I never liked her anyway. (*FRDG*, Oct. 18, 1893)

The *Daily Evening News* reported that Mrs. Downing's statement, "I never liked her anyway," caused laughter in the courtroom. As Bragg rested Stephen's case:

> [He] stated to the court that Bertha Manchester, his most important witness had been murdered since the suit was brought and Mr. Reed wanted to know what necessitated continual reference to that unfortunate affair, to which Mr. Bragg replied that he wanted the court to know that it was no fault of his if Bertha was not present to testify. (*FRDG*, Oct. 18, 1893)

Reed now took over for Mary Jane's case and immediately called her to the stand. She confirmed Stephen's description of her having been a domestic at the Manchester house. Her brother Samuel had suggested she apply for the position, but no details were given as to how Samuel knew about the Manchesters. Although she did not elaborate, Mary Jane said she had been in bad health since the birth of her son. She testified that, until Alexander was born, "there was little or no trouble." She claimed the first absence of three days was due to her being sick. She felt Manchester's behavior was due to the influence of Stephen's sister and family.

Her story about the baby crying was a bit different. Stephen had said he was not in the same room with Mary Jane and the baby, but Mary Jane testified that Stephen "went to the window to raise it." She added, "I told him if he touched that child I would kill him." According to her, Stephen was so enraged he frothed at the mouth. This scared her so much that she felt she had to leave the house. Therefore, she went across the road to Charles Reed's house for the night.

She disagreed with Stephen about the times she left, saying that, in each case, he asked to do so. She stayed away three months after the crying incident.

While perhaps not as animated on the stand as Stephen, she certainly held back no words. Following is her description of the rooster affair:

> I was washing the milk cans and heard the child scream. I looked and saw him lash the child with a horsewhip and ran out, and picked the child up and was badly bruised and cut with the lash.

He went for me with a lump of wood but I dodged it. I took the child and left him again and did not go back for about eight months. I was advised about the matter and went back to live with him. He was worse than ever and abused me. Once he threw a milk can at me and I dodged it. Then he slapped my face and left the prints of his fingers on my ear and cheek. My head swelled up and I was in pain for a long time. (*FRDG*, Oct. 18, 1893)

The *Daily Evening News* reported that the person who advised Mary Jane was Judge Blaisdell, best known for presiding at the inquest held for the Borden murders and at the preliminary hearing for Lizzie Borden. During this absence, she lived with a Mrs. Goss.

Mary Jane stated over and over that she was abused. Some of it was psychological, with Stephen saying that he would have to have his sister Nancy come over to show Mary Jane how to boil potatoes.

James Whittles said he saw finger marks on Mary Jane's face. Louisa Greaves testified she once saw Mary Jane's face swollen. A Mrs. Kennedy and Mrs. Alice Gorse said they saw a serious injury on Mary Jane's shoulder.

Thirteen-year-old Edwin Whittles, the sole family survivor of the Watuppa Pond tragedy, testified he was in the Manchester house during the incident when the chair was pulled from under Mary Jane. He said both Manchester's sister Nancy and daughter Bertha had to hold Stephen back.

Thomas Broughton testified he worked on the Manchester farm for a period after the baby was born. He said Stephen had a "rough temper," although he was unaware of trouble between the couple. Perhaps in connection with the comment on Stephen's temper, Broughton said he had not come to court to testify against Stephen "in order to get square with him for the loss of a tooth." This comment also resulted in laughter in the courtroom.

The two counsels then presented their closing arguments. Mary Jane's attorney, Milton Reed, pointed out the pathos involved. Stephen Manchester had lost a daughter in a brutal murder, while Mary Jane saw her brother, sister-in-law, and two nephews die in a single afternoon. But back to the matter at hand, he stated that Stephen was "an old, wealthy, Yankee farmer" and Mary Jane "was not a jaunty adventuress." The troubles within the marriage were intensified by "mischief-maker" Nancy Downing. He said the evidence clearly indicated that Stephen had no use for Mary Jane or Alexander. Stephen was heartless. Mary Jane was forgiving but afraid of Stephen. The rooster was more important to Stephen than was Alexander.

Stephen claimed to be quite ill when Mary Jane came back to the house for the last time but, according to Reed, "[he] was not too sick to walk down to Lawyer Bragg's office the next day and apply for a divorce."

Reed asked for Mary Jane's petition to be granted, with costs. He further requested that Mary Jane receive alimony and custody of Alexander, along with support for the child. Reed said he could not at that time request a specific amount and asked that the court investigate Manchester's financial position to decide a proper sum.

As one might expect, lawyer Bragg did not leap to his feet to endorse Reed's requests. As to Manchester's actions, as a dairy farmer, Manchester could sleep only between nine o'clock and midnight and could not afford to be disturbed during those hours. Bragg's client neither foamed at the mouth nor acted like "a raving maniac." He "lightly struck" Alexander during the rooster incident.

As to Mary Jane's witnesses, Bragg said, only James Whittles specifically referenced seeing any finger marks upon her face. There had been no fighting and quarreling between the couple. Manchester's wife was "a full blooded, hot tempered woman." (It would seem this last sentence somewhat contradicts the assessment made in the previous one.)

Reed claimed that Mary Jane's case alleging cruelty had failed. Further, Stephen's abandonment claims were verified, as there is no doubt that Mary Jane lived with him only eighteen months out of the eight years the couple had been married. Because of this, she should not receive one third of Stephen's estate. Stephen did want custody of Alexander.

At least by the standards of today, a divorce decree by the court certainly would seem in order. Mary Jane claimed Stephen struck her and, although he denied it and no one witnessed any such battery, she had produced four witnesses that asserted they saw her with facial injuries. Although Stephen claimed to desire custody of Alexander, there is little evidence he had any interest in the boy.

Despite what would seem to have been sufficient evidence that a divorce decree was in order, Judge Hopkins reserved his decision.

It so happened that the Manchester divorce case was heard at the conclusion of the September session of the Superior Court. On October 19, Judge Hopkins gave his decisions on several cases he had heard during the session. Obviously, the standards for divorce in Fall River in 1893 were much more stringent than today, as the judge dismissed the libels of both parties in the Manchester case. He ordered that Stephen pay court costs. This may have been because the judge thought that Stephen did strike Mary Jane but the more likely deciding factor was simply that Stephen was the only one of the two who had the means to pay the costs.

With Hopkins's dismissals, the Manchesters remained married. No other actions for divorce were brought, so the couple remained so for life.

Louis Quarry had been held briefly in June as a suspect in the Manchester case. The arrest of Jose Correa (de Mello) on June 1 essentially cleared Quarry of the serious charge, but on that same day he was convicted of vagrancy and sentenced to one month in the House of Corrections.

Although not originally from the area, upon his release, he stayed in Fall River. However, his habits were not affected during his forced vacation time with the state. He was again arrested for vagrancy and, on October 25, was sentenced to one year at the state farm in Bridgewater, Massachusetts.

CHAPTER 10
FINALITY

After de Mello's arraignment, the newspapers had no reports of defense counsel being assigned by the Court. A session of the Superior Court met in November, but the case was not then heard. Finally, with the beginning of a new year, movement finally took place.

Attorney Swift had waited until the day of the arraignment of de Mello (then Correiro) to submit a plea of misnomer. If his intention was to buy time, perhaps in order that the Portuguese community would raise funds to hire an attorney for their countryman, the ploy worked. However, as it happened, the previous report that the local Portuguese had stopped donating to his cause was true. De Mello's father also declined to come to the U.S. to aid in his son's defense. Now, in January of 1894, with apparently no other options, Judge John Hopkins once again appointed Swift & Grime as de Mello's defense counsel, meaning that the county would have to foot the bill. According to the *Daily Herald*, the firm accepted, albeit with little apparent enthusiasm.

With no counsel during the period after his arraignment, there is no reason to believe any backdoor legal wrangling had occurred. This was in complete contrast to the Borden case, where Lizzie Borden had counsel from the day of the murders onward and much back-and-forth discussion took place before the trial began. However, here in the Manchester case, it is quite likely that Knowlton had discussed Commonwealth options with Attorney General Pillsbury to move things forward when the opportunity arose.

Swift & Grime were familiar with the case, since they had represented de Mello at the preliminary hearing and his arraignment. Given the confession de Mello made to the police and his leading them to the site of the watch, one could deduce that these seasoned attorneys would see no way out for their client.

The *Daily Herald* reported on the appointment of Swift & Grime in their January 6, 1894, issue. (The other two dailies did not report on the event.) But, in the same article, the newspaper claimed that no trial date had yet been set and would require a special assignment of the Superior Court, with a three-judge panel selected. However, the newspaper already predicted it would be unlikely a trial would take place. The newspaper stated:

> From a talk with the prisoner's lawyers, it is gathered that the line of defence will be that Bertha Manchester was the first assailant, as it was attempted to do by the testimony at the district court. If an agreement is reached between the commonwealth and the attorneys for De Mello the latter may be sentenced at any time. Otherwise a special assignment will be made for the trial, which, at best, is not likely to happen for some time to come.
>
> A dispatch from Taunton intimates that the district attorney has accepted the proposition of the defense to a plea of guilty of manslaughter. This dispatch says that Correiro will probably go before Judge [Henry] Braley on Monday to retract his former plea, plead guilty to manslaughter, and be sentenced at once. (*FRDH*, Jan. 6, 1894)

The *Daily Herald*, as it turned out, was quite accurate in their prediction. Upon being named counsel, Swift & Grime immediately consulted with their client and informed him of his options. One of them, obviously, would be to change his plea from not-guilty to that of guilty of a lesser offense than first-degree murder, a charge he might have been convicted of if he went to trial. Of course, even if he wished to plea down, the prosecution had to agree to it. Within two days, the drama had ended. On January 8, 1893, the fate of Jose Correa de Mello would be decided:

> Jose Correia De Mello, the self-confessed murderer of Bertha May Manchester, arrived in this city on the noon train in charge of Isaac Carrier, assistant keeper of the Taunton jail. He was taken at once to the court house. He and his counsel were in the consultation room together till 2:15 when brought into court. He was not handcuffed, but walked in front of the keeper and took his place on the dock. (*FRDH*, Jan. 8, 1894)

The *Daily Herald* reporter noted that, after several months in prison, de Mello "looks fatter and stronger than he did when arraigned in the lower court." Despite all the publicity the case had received, there was no crowd in the courtroom. The reporter opined, given that the *Daily Herald* had already reported on what likely would happen, that the paucity of people in the gallery was because there would be no drama. He felt it necessary to add, "affording a respectable contrast with another murder trial still fresh in mind."

> In the superior court this afternoon Jose de Mello was arraigned for the murder of Bertha Manchester. Lawyer Da Terra was sworn as interpreter.
>
> Mello was asked if he wished to change his plea of not guilty, and replied that he would "plead guilty to murder in the second degree."
>
> Judge Braley then asked District Attorney Knowlton if the plea was acceptable to the commonwealth, and Mr. Knowlton addressed the court. (*FRDG*, Jan. 8, 1894)

Knowlton presented the facts of the case and the evidence collected. Because by all appearances it was Bertha who first seized the axe and attempted to attack de Mello, Knowlton said it was not "probable that the state could prove a case of murder in the first degree." (It seems strange that no one had ever considered that, being challenged by the larger and stronger Bertha, it was de Mello who grabbed the axe from the woodbox. After all, de Mello had no apparent injuries.)

Knowlton told the court that if the attack had happened at night rather than during the day, as was the case here, the charge might have been otherwise:

> There is a technicality in the law which makes it possible to allege that malice prompts a crime of this kind if committed at night time. (*FRDG*, Jan. 8, 1894)

Also complicating matters, Knowlton said, is that one of the state's most important witnesses, Captain Philip Harrington, had died, crippling the state's case. Although not stated by Knowlton, it would be assumed that Jacintho Muniz Machado's death would also hinder the government's case:

> I have ... decided after consultation with the attorney general, and at the solicitation of the police of this city, and by reason of my own judgment, to accept this plea of murder in the second degree.
>
> I think it very doubtful if a jury would bring in a verdict of guilty on a charge of murder in the first degree. I accept this plea in behalf of the commonwealth, and move for a sentence. (*FRDG*, Jan. 8, 1894)

Then, for the defense, lawyer Swift addressed the court. He and de Mello had certainly agreed beforehand to Knowlton's charge, so there was no attempt to argue against it. However, he obviously felt the duty to attempt to mitigate the sentence. He told the court that all indications were that, before coming to America, de Mello was of "a peaceful disposition." Swift added that de Mello "has found people here who have interested themselves in his behalf." He thanked those who had done so. He added, "I think the government is quite conclusively convinced that he is not of a murderous disposition." In conclusion, Swift said, "Inasmuch as nothing more can be done in his behalf, I have nothing more to say."

Knowlton again rose, saying, "I intended to say that my course in this matter has been recommended by the police."

Before sentencing, Judge Braley asked de Mello if he desired to say anything. Da Terra told his client what the judge had said. De Mello's response was, "Have mercy on me."

After only a moment's hesitation, Judge Braley wrote on a piece of paper and handed it to Court Clerk Simeon Borden, who read the note. De Mello's one request would not be granted.

> Jose Correiro [sic] de Mello, harken to the sentence which the court has awarded you. The court having considered the offense of which you are now stand convicted, orders that you be committed to the states prison for the remainder of your natural life, one day of which is to be solitary confinement and the remainder at hard labor. (*FRDG*, Jan. 8, 1894)

Jose de Mello was immediately taken from the courtroom and escorted by the sheriff to the train station. The two boarded the 3:39 train for Taunton and sat in the second car. Unlike Lizzie Borden, whose movements to and from court proceedings were followed closely by the citizens of Fall River, the transportation of de Mello drew little attention. At first, few people at the station recognized de Mello. But once someone pointed him out, the crowd tried to get a glimpse of him on the train. De Mello's re-incarceration in the Taunton jail would be brief. On January 11, he was transported to the Charlestown State Prison in Boston to serve his life sentence.

CHAPTER 11
DE MELLO VS. BORDEN

Bertha Manchester was murdered on May 30, 1893. The trial of Lizzie Borden began less than a week later, on June 5. Some in Fall River thought the killer of Bertha Manchester might be the same person who killed the Bordens. Marshal Hilliard assured the public that this was not the case, especially with the quick arrest of Jose Correiro (later to be called de Mello). Even those supporting the innocence of Lizzie Borden did not think the same person was responsible for all three murders. While the murders were not believed to be connected, many still felt they had a common point of comparison: the treatment of the accused.

As we saw in the chapter titled "The Wait," a member of the Fall River Portuguese community protested the treatment of de Mello to the *Fall River Daily Herald*. Following is his complete letter from the newspaper's June 13, 1893, edition:

A STRONG PROTEST

A Friend of Correiro Says He Has Been Treated Harshly

Mr. Editor: Sir:—I wish to draw the attention of the public to the case of the unfortunate Correiro, now locked up in the central station. I wish to protest against the indignities to which he is now submitted, and, by contrast, to show HERALD readers that there is a law for the rich and respected and another for the poor and helpless.

When Miss Borden was suspected of committing the double murders which appalled the civilized world, she was taken to the station in a closed carriage and back to her home at night. She was finally arrested, very delicately, very tenderly. She was placed in the matron's room. She was favored by hotel fare, bouquets, clerical friends, visitors and to top it all ceaseless howl from the "hill" and the "press" arose about the outrage and injustice to which was submitted.

Now another horrible murder; this time one victim instead of two. Correiro is suspected; he hears the police are looking for him; he walks into the station to give himself up. He is immediately thrown–that is the word–thrown into a cell, a dark cell, if you please. That is two weeks ago, and from that day to this not a soul has he seen, not a soul can he see; he is practically condemned, fed on prison fare, locked in solitary confinement. He cannot speak a word of English; his relatives have asked permission to see him, to speak to him, and were denied. There have been no bouquets, no flowers, no words of sympathy, no protest from the hill. We wish to ask the police department why this distinction?

A responsible Portuguese citizen asked the head of the department today if he could speak to Correiro. "Yes," said the captain, "if you speak English so that I may understand you." But Correiro cannot understand English. I wish to know if the captain was present at every interview Lizzie Borden had with her friends. Why, Mr. Captain, this distinction? Does money make it? Again the gentleman asked if the prisoner had counsel; he was informed that Nicholas Hatheway had been appointed. We visited the office of Mr. Hatheway and was surprised to learn that Mr. Hatheway knew nothing of the case and had not been engaged. What does it mean? In the name of justice, in the name of decency, in the name of common humanity, we request the authorities to be just and not so blinded by pomp and power, and so dazzled by the brilliancy of wealth and influence that you forget the justice which the constitution of your nation guarantees shall exist between man and man even to the meanest of our kind.

JOSEPH M. CHAVES.

As is typically done by those making impassioned pleas, Chaves may have overstated his case a bit. As previously stated in "The Wait," the police captain referenced, Philip Harrington, upon reading Chaves's letter, said that Correiro could have visitors, but they would be limited by those involved in his case, to avoid an influx of curiosity seekers.

But it was not just the Portuguese who early on thought de Mello was being treated differently than had been Lizzie Borden. On the same day the *Daily Herald* published Chaves's letter, the *Fall River Daily Globe* commented on an article printed in the *Providence Journal*:

WHY THIS DISCRIMINATION?

While the circumstantial evidence against the Portuguese suspect, Correiro, is considered strong by the Fall River police who are engaged in the investigation of the Manchester murder case, he should be subjected to no peculiar hardships because of his apparent lack of friends and the unusual isolation in which he failed to understand the English language seems to have placed him. Every effort must be made, of course, to secure and convict the dastardly assassin of Miss Bertha Manchester, but it is not necessary to treat Correiro like a condemned criminal already, simply because no other suspected individual is in sight. — [Prov. Journal.]

The Journal's comments are right, and the difference in the treatment which has been accorded this "suspect" and another charged with a similar crime, while in custody of the local authorities is marked. There ought not to be any distinction made in matters of this kind as the law doesn't recognize such. It presumes that all shall be treated alike. (June 13, 1893)

The trial of Lizzie Borden was in session at the time these articles were published. On June 12, the Superior Court justices in that trial ruled that the inquest testimony of Lizzie Borden would not be read into evidence. Her testimony had been rambling and arguably anyone hearing it might well have been led to more questions about her guilt than by the testimony of others at the trial. Therefore, the exclusion of this testimony was a major victory for the defense. While the *Daily Globe* had commented briefly on the *Providence Journal* article, the decision to exclude Lizzie Borden's inquest testimony led the *Daily Globe* to expand on the unequal treatment of de Mello:

HOW ABOUT THE CORREIRO CASE?

And now as to Correiro. Is he guilty of the murder of Bertha Manchester, and taking the ruling of the court in the Borden trial, as a criterion to judge by, have not the police authorities deprived him of his personal rights in seeking to extort information damaging to himself, from this man, when, to all intents and purposes he was in duress.

There are some features of his case which bear a striking resemblance to that of Lizzie Borden. One of the strongest points is made by those who scout the theory that the latter is guilty of the crime for which she was indicted, is that no blood was found on her person or garments. It is contended that it would have been impossible for any one to commit a crime of the nature of that which ended the lives of Andrew Borden and his wife, without being literally covered with the blood of the victims.

Yet the murder at the Manchester house was of precisely the same character, and all the blood that the argus-eyed police have discerned on Correiro's clothes, so far as they have been willing to admit at least, is a single spot on his shirt front, and for the presence of which he is reported to have offered a plausible explanation.

But what is of more importance in considering this matter, is whether or not the authorities have not made the same blunder in dealing with Correiro that the Superior Court has decided they made in the other instance.

At the time he was taken into the office at the Central Station, and questioned and probed by the Mayor and marshal, his arrest, if the public has been rightly informed, was practically decided upon. The police were at that moment, in their own belief, in possession of evidence of an incriminating character sufficient to justify such action. It is true the star chamber proceedings then instituted did not assume the dignity of a formal inquest, and a court which would exclude statements made by a suspect at a hearing of the latter kind, might conclude to admit what was said at a different sort of inquisition.

To the mind of a layman however, this might be regarded as distinction without a difference so far as the preservation of the rights of the accused is concerned. It might be law but not common sense, and as good a lawyer as ex-Gov. Robinson [Lizzie Borden's attorney] contended in his argument a few days ago that "common sense was better than law under some circumstances." If anything, Correiro didn't have as fair a show as Lizzie Borden. Before she gave the testimony so damaging to herself at the inquest, she had been officially apprised of the fact that she was suspected. It doesn't appear, however, that any intimation of this kind had been given to this friendless Portuguese or that he was warned of the fact that what he would say might be used against him.

We don't pretend to know just what took place at the marshal's office while the suspected man was on the rack from 7 in the evening until 4 in the morning. But the ridiculous policy which the authorities have pursued in attempting to make a solemn and oppressive secret of nearly everything they have done in connection with this case, leaves the public free to draw its own inferences, and reach its own conclusions. Hence, as we assume that Correiro was not advised, to quote the classical simile of Alderman Beattie, that on the occasion in question, the sword of Damocles was suspended over head.

We assume, also, that he wasn't warned that any indiscreet or contradictory statement he might make, would be to his detriment in the event of his being put on trial for his life. If these assumptions are correct, and taking the rulings in the Borden case into consideration, the question arises, haven't the authorities commenced by laying the foundation of an important part of their case against Correiro on quick sands, as the court has decided they did in the Borden case? It is to be hoped that they know where they are at, but until they make their position clear, the public will have its misgivings in view of recent events. (June 17, 1893)

The *Daily Globe* doubled down on this by printing the June 18 article displayed in "The Wait" regarding what they felt had been Correiro's forced confession.

All the above articles appeared in mid-June, at a point when de Mello was being held for his preliminary hearing. As such, they do not address the treatment of the two defendants during the entire time of their incarcerations. Before doing so, let us summarize the events surrounding the two crimes.

The Borden Murders

Andrew and Abby Borden were killed on August 4, 1892, at 92 Second Street in Fall River. This part of Second Street had once been relatively high class but had deteriorated to some extent. There were, however, still some relics of past glory. Mayor Edward Buffinton had lived in a large house at 90 Second Street. He had since died, but his family still occupied the property. Wealthy contractor Southard Miller lived across the street. His house was divided into a duplex, with his daughter and her husband, Dr. Seabury Bowen, occupying the northern half of the building.

Andrew Borden had purchased the two-family house at 92 Second Street in 1872. He converted it into a middle- to upper-middle-class single-family house. But Andrew Borden, now sixty-nine years old, had, over the years, amassed much greater wealth than this house would indicate.

Just after 11 o'clock, Lizzie Borden called up to the attic room of the Borden servant, Bridget Sullivan, telling her to come down immediately, as Andrew Borden had been murdered. Lizzie then sent Bridget across the street to get Dr. Bowen. When Bridget arrived, Bowen's wife told her he was out on his rounds but would return home shortly. Bridget returned to the Borden house with the message, whereupon Lizzie told her to fetch Lizzie's friend, Alice Russell, who lived a few streets away. Soon afterward, Mrs. Adelaide Churchill (the daughter of the late mayor) looked southward out of her kitchen window. She noticed a forlorn-looking Lizzie standing just inside the rear doorway on the north side of the Borden house. She asked Lizzie if something was wrong. Lizzie told Mrs. Churchill to come over right away, as someone had killed her father. Mrs. Churchill did so. Lizzie then sent her to get a doctor. Mrs. Churchill went down the street to Hall's stable where her hired man had gone. Finding him, she sent him for a doctor. During her conversation with some men who were in front of the stable, a local newsdealer, John Cunningham, walked by and happened to hear about some type of altercation at the Borden house. It seemed serious enough that he walked down the street to a paint store and called Marshal Hilliard as well as the local newspapers.

Mrs. Churchill went back to the Borden house and, about this time, Dr. Bowen returned from his rounds. His wife told him to go to the Borden house, which he did. About the same time, Bridget returned, followed shortly by Alice Russell. Bowen confirmed Andrew was dead; he had been murdered. He had Mrs. Churchill and Bridget Sullivan get a sheet with which he covered the body. Soon thereafter, Officer George Allen arrived. Cunningham had not known that a murder had taken place, so Allen was not prepared for the sight of Andrew, lying dead with his face hacked many times. After briefly looking around the first floor, he returned to the police station to apprise the marshal.

Lizzie asked Bowen to send a telegram to her sister Emma, who was staying with friends in Fairhaven, about twenty miles away. Bowen left to do so. Lizzie had told everyone that her stepmother, Abby, had received a note and, as a result, had gone to visit a sick friend. Now, however, she said she thought she had heard Abby return and asked the women to look for her. Mrs. Churchill and Bridget Sullivan knew Abby was not in her bedroom, because they had gone there to get the sheet. So they went up the front stairs to the guest room where they found Abby, also dead. They came back downstairs and told Lizzie and Alice.

Bowen now returned from sending the telegram. Told by Mrs. Churchill of what they had found, Bowen went upstairs to the guest room. He confirmed Abby was dead, although at first did not seem to realize she had also been murdered in a similar attack as Andrew had suffered.

Now, in response to Officer Allen returning to the station, two policemen arrived, Deputy County Sheriff Francis Wixon and Fall River Officer Patrick Doherty. Of course, both had expected to find one body, not two. Now confronted with a second death, Doherty walked around the corner and phoned Hilliard. Many more policemen were now sent, arriving at various times.

Officer Allen obviously did not suspect Lizzie Borden, since he searched for an intruder in the first-floor closets. Lizzie was interviewed by a few other policemen, who also did not suspect her. Assistant Marshal John Fleet then showed up. Interviewing Lizzie, he apparently also, at first, assumed the perpetrator was an intruder. But he seemed to have a problem with Lizzie's story that her father had been killed while she had been in the barn loft for twenty minutes. Lizzie's tone about her stepmother also gave him pause. He left Lizzie and went to the yard to instruct the officers as to their assignments. Meanwhile, Officer William Medley arrived. He, too, interviewed Lizzie and also seemed not to believe her about the trip to the barn loft. He went to the barn and inspected the floor of the loft. He satisfied himself that the dust there had not been disturbed by foot traffic. (Later testimonies contradicted Medley's assertion.) A half-hour or so later, Officer Philip Harrington interviewed Lizzie and found her story wanting.

After completing instructions to his officers in the back yard, Fleet returned to the Borden house and interviewed Lizzie a second time. At this point, he must have had a strong suspicion of her as he ordered a general search of the entire house. Two intact hatchets were found as well as a hatchet head in which only a stub of a handle remained. Fleet returned to the station to apprise Hilliard.

In the afternoon, a large group of police searched the barn. At 3:00, the stomachs of the victims were removed during a partial autopsy. They were later sent to Professor Edward Wood at the Harvard Medical School. Wood determined no poisons were present in them.

The funeral was held Saturday and, just afterward, a thorough search of the Borden house and property was undertaken. That night, Mayor Coughlin and Marshal Hilliard visited the house. The inhabitants, which now comprised Lizzie, Emma, Bridget, and John Morse, an uncle who had been visiting but was not there when the murders were committed. Coughlin told them that, for their own safety, they should not leave the house, as there had been a city-wide frenzy resulting from the murders. Lizzie asked Coughlin if anyone in the house was suspected, whereupon Coughlin admitted to Lizzie that she was.

Sunday morning, Emma and Alice Russell saw Lizzie tear up a dress in the kitchen. Although neither saw her throw the dress into the kitchen stove, there is no doubt she did so.

About 10:00 a.m. on Monday, several police again searched the Borden cellar. Nothing new was found, but the handleless hatchet that had been noticed on Thursday was now taken to the station. At about noon, a warrant was issued for the arrest of Lizzie Borden, but was not served.

An inquest into the deaths of the Bordens began on Tuesday. Lizzie testified that day and the next as well, returning to stay in her house in between. She was called again on Thursday, whereupon a witness identified her as the woman who entered a drug store on the day before the murders. (She had asked to purchase highly poisonous prussic acid but had been denied because she had no prescription.) At that point, Lizzie was taken to the matron's room. (She had not heard the witness.) While she was kept there, Marshal Rufus Hilliard and District Attorney Hosea Knowlton, who had been the questioner at the inquest, telephoned Borden family lawyer Andrew Jennings to tell him they were about to arrest Lizzie. Jennings hurried to the police station. For some reason, the warrant previously issued was ignored. However, the police now presented a new warrant.

Lizzie stayed in the matron's room overnight. After being charged the next day, she was transported to the county jail in Taunton. She was brought back to Fall River about two weeks later for the preliminary hearing. It began on a Monday, but the counsels needed more time, and the proceeding was continued until Thursday. It was decided that it was too much trouble to take Lizzie back to Taunton and return within two days to Fall River, so she was again housed in the matron's room, not a cell, in the Fall River police station, for three days. The preliminary hearing lasted more than a week. Each day after court, Lizzie was returned to the matron's room. During that time, there appears to have been no restrictions, other than those imposed by Lizzie, as to who might visit with her. Besides Jennings, her sister, uncle, clergy, and friends called on her constantly during that time.

After the lengthy preliminary hearing, Judge Blaisdell found her "probably guilty," and she was returned for incarceration in Taunton until her trial the following June.

THE MANCHESTER MURDER

The events and procedures surrounding the Manchester murder just after this crime were quite different from those during the Borden investigation. When the first policeman arrived at the Borden house, he did not even know there had been a murder. The second officer to arrive, Doherty, thought one person had been killed. He then had to call Hilliard and advise him that there were two bodies. Bertha Manchester's body was found by her twelve-year-old brother, Freddie. He immediately alerted his father, who drove to the police station to report the crime. A delegation of police, along with Medical Examiner Dr. William Dolan, were immediately sent to the Manchester house and could hit the ground running with respect to an investigation.

It was clear that Bertha had been attacked in the kitchen, apparently with an axe or hatchet. An axe, later identified by Stephen as the one kept in the kitchen woodbox, was quickly located in the yard near the house. The first suspects were the males inhabiting the house: Stephen, his son Freddie, and farm hand John Tonsall. But all three had seen Bertha as they left the farm for the daily milk route. They had been together several hours thereafter, finding Bertha upon their return. This precluded any simple resolution to the case.

Given the era in which Bertha's murder occurred, the next suspect in line would be a member of a minority group, most likely a Portuguese. Stephen had recently had such an employee, a man he called Manuel. Stephen acknowledged there had been some friction between the two over the rate of pay but admitted that he was a hard taskmaster and often had disputes with his workers. As a result, most did not stay with him long. He kept records of his payments to them but was not fussy about exact identification. When the subject of "Manuel" came up, Stephen said he did not think the young man would commit such a crime.

In the Borden case, no clear-cut evidence was found. There were two intact hatchets and one hatchet head found in the cellar, but there was no blood on any of them. Some strange dust on the handleless hatchet led police to think it might have been washed and then doctored to look as if it had not been handled. But even if that were the case, neither it, nor the other two hatchets, could be directly tied to any individual. Police found no blood on Lizzie (or Bridget, for that matter). If an intruder committed the crime, no one had seen him come or go. There was neither any evidence of an intruder being in the house, nor did it appear to have been ransacked or robbed. In fact, absolutely nothing had been disturbed.

Similarly, there was no direct evidence found in the Manchester case. The house clearly had been robbed and ransacked, but the forensic science of the time could not tie this activity to a particular person. No one had seen anyone come or go on the property. This, coupled with the finding that Stephen, Freddie, and John were not suspects, clearly meant an intruder must have committed the crime. This narrowed the field to the 80,000 inhabitants of the city, although the number was much higher if they considered that a drifter could have been the culprit. (As we saw, Lewis Quarry was just such a suspect for a brief time.)

There had been no other similar break-ins in the area, so the police concluded that the Manchester house was not selected at random—the perpetrator must have targeted the house because he thought or knew money or valuables were kept there. This, in turn, is what led them to concentrate on farmhands hired by Stephen. Portuguese coming to the city were often told to see certain individuals who were knowledgeable on employment that might be available. By contacting them, they found that "Manuel" was Jose de Mello, or Jose Correiro, as he was then known. Police quickly found other Portuguese who knew about de Mello. However, by then, de Mello had left Fall River for parts unknown.

Police soon got a tip that de Mello was in Taunton. They brought in his uncle, Jacintho Muniz Machado, and threatened him if he did not go to Taunton and bring his nephew in the same day. According to the newspapers, Machado was told by the police that they wanted to see de Mello about a man who had stolen a horse. This was not confirmed by the police, but it makes sense the police did not send Machado to Taunton to ask de Mello to come to Fall River because he was suspected of murder.

Once at the police station, de Mello was grilled unmercifully for hours. He could not speak English, so he had to struggle through an interpreter. He was unfamiliar with American police practices. He certainly had had no lawyer before this time and was not offered one by the police. In these days long before the Miranda rights law, it is unlikely he was apprised of any rights he might have.

As far as can be discerned, at the time they told Machado to bring de Mello back to Fall River, all they knew about de Mello was that he had bought a pair of shoes before leaving town. They brought in Joseph Lacroix, the store owner, and Manuel Sousa, the witness to the purchase, while grilling de Mello. The two men identified de Mello and described the method of purchase, which contradicted his story. Based on that discrepancy, he was arrested. Newspaper articles led one to believe that the police did not know the coins used to buy the shoes were stolen from Bertha Manchester's bedroom until after de Mello was arrested, but there is no way to know that for sure. However, it is an important point, since, without that knowledge, the police did not have enough to arrest de Mello as there was no other direct connection between the shoe purchase and Bertha Manchester, and no other evidence against de Mello whatsoever.

It was noted in Chapter Six that the *Fall River Daily Herald* claimed that one of its reporters was at the police station just before midnight on June 6 when it so happened that a police wagon drove up. Captains Desmond, Connors, and Doherty exited the wagon, with de Mello handcuffed to Doherty. According to the newspaper, the police then told the reporter that de Mello had now admitted to committing the murder and had taken the three officers to the spot the watch and handbag had been hidden. De Mello had been arrested early on the morning of June 4. He was arraigned the next day. It was thus more than three days after he turned himself in, about sixty hours after his arrest, and more than thirty-six hours after his arraignment, that de Mello was seen by the reporter. Clearly, at no time during that span had an attorney been afforded to de Mello. Given the rules, or lack thereof, involved in police interrogation in 1893, the absence of counsel and ignorance of the English language and American laws, it might well be deduced that de Mello's confession was beaten out of him, not physically, but psychologically.

Let us now consider the treatment of Lizzie Borden and Jose de Mello, broken down by equivalent time periods.

The Crimes

Lizzie Borden

When Officer George Allen arrived at the Borden house, he assumed Andrew Borden had been killed by an intruder. (He was unaware of the murder of Abby Borden.) This was based on the location of the Borden property in a middle-class area of the city. Further, he found that the only inhabitants present at the time of the murder were Lizzie Borden and Bridget Sullivan. Both were distraught and neither had any visible blood on their persons nor any other sign of involvement.

It should be pointed out that Allen was not a regular police officer. On the day of the murders, many in the police force were at their annual summer outing at Rocky Point, Rhode Island. When the call came in to City Marshal Hilliard, no regular officer was available, and he was unaware that a murder had been committed. The only available person to send was fifty-four-year-old Allen, whose daily job was, and always had been, to move prisoners from place to place.

Allen's assumption that an intruder committed the crimes does not seem unreasonable, but his actions upon making that assumption were atrocious. He looked only in the first-floor closets for a possible lurking intruder. Had he looked on the second floor, he would have also found Abby Borden. Further, if he thought it possible an intruder was still lurking, why would he not look on every floor? And, since he did not, should not he at least tell the inhabitants to exit the house for their own safety until more police arrived?

Allen did have the presence of mind to corral neighborhood resident Charles Sawyer to stand inside the back entranceway and not let anyone in except the police or doctors. But while standing there, Sawyer saw that the door to the cellar was unlocked. He locked it in case someone was still in the basement.

Allen could have avoided all this by telling Sawyer to go to a local store to call the marshal (as Cunningham had earlier done). In acting that way, Allen could have stayed at the Borden house until reinforcements arrived.

But if one is going to criticize Allen, it should also be noted that the next few officers who arrived also thought an intruder was the culprit. Unlike Allen, they did not check the house *at all* for an intruder.

Jose de Mello

The scene at the Manchester farm was quite different from that at the Bordens' respecting the arrival of the police. Upon discovering that his daughter had been murdered, Stephen Manchester drove to the station to report the crime. When police arrived at the farm, they searched the area and confirmed no intruder was present, although it would be deduced that they suspected this beforehand. But Stephen Manchester was their first suspect. It was not until it was confirmed he was with his son and farmhand all day that he was cleared.

We see the difference here between class and gender. Because Lizzie Borden was of reasonably high class and a woman, the early-arriving policemen did not consider her as a suspect. Stephen Manchester, a male of a lesser class, was considered immediately. One might argue that upper-class women are far less likely to brutally kill a family member than is a male of a lesser class, and, therefore, the initial assumptions were not invalid. But these assumptions, while not greatly hindering the Manchester case, certainly did so regarding the Borden murders.

Suspicion

Lizzie Borden

Given the nature of the Borden murders, one might understand the initial response of the police. But once suspicion was focused on a single individual, the cases completely diverge.

Police began to suspect Lizzie Borden less than half an hour after Allen had first reported the murder of Andrew Borden. There is no question that suspicion of her was high by shortly after noon when Fleet began a search of the house that would seem to go far beyond looking for evidence of an intruder. For example, Fleet took Bridget Sullivan to the attic where she unlocked the various doors. Clearly, by now Fleet realized that nothing in the house had been stolen or disturbed, so there was no reason for an intruder to have put himself in jeopardy by going all the way up to the attic. And, just as certainly, an intruder would not have had access to the locked rooms.

The house search that day revealed no evidence. Once the police departed, the inhabitants were left on their own, except for three policemen who remained in the yard to guard unauthorized entry to the house. About 8:30 that night, Officer Joseph Hyde saw Lizzie Borden and Alice Russell go down to the cellar. The two soon left but, about fifteen minutes later, Hyde saw Lizzie go back down to the cellar alone. He saw her enter the washroom on the east end of the basement. She bent down out of his sight to do something, soon leaving to go back up the stairs.

There was no search on the next day, Friday. On Saturday, a thorough search was done throughout the house and barn. That night, the mayor and marshal visited the Borden house and, while there, Lizzie was told by the mayor she was a suspect. Sunday morning, Lizzie burned the dress.

From just after noon on the day of the murders until she testified at the inquest five days later, there is no record or later testimony indicating the police attempted to further question Lizzie Borden. Of course, she had a lawyer, Andrew Jennings, but the police still had a right to question her in his presence. The lack of further questioning might have been because District Attorney Hosea Knowlton knew he would be able to question her in a somewhat unfettered manner, without her lawyer being present, at the inquest.

That inquest was held the following Tuesday, Wednesday, and Thursday. On each of the days, the marshal sent a wagon for Lizzie. She returned home the first two of the days the same way. (She was arrested at the end of the inquest on Thursday.) Other witnesses were left to make their way to the courtroom by their own devices. And, it will be remembered, this was done not just for an upper-middle-class woman but the woman the police felt likely killed her father and stepmother.

JOSE DE MELLO

Jose de Mello began this case with a condition he could never be rid of—he was Portuguese. As an example, it might be noted that when the police first thought an intruder might have killed the Bordens, they asked Lizzie if her father employed any Portuguese on his farm in Swansea. The police had little, if anything, to go on once they ruled out Stephen Manchester as a suspect, his dismissal occurring the same day as the murders. Stephen's current farmhand was teenager John Tonsall. He was cleared by the police the same time as Stephen, since the two shared the alibi of being together, with Stephen's young son Freddie, the entire morning of the murder. Asked if he had hired any Portuguese farmhands lately, Manchester came up with the name Manuel, although he never worried much about recording the workers' actual names. Later, at the preliminary hearing, Stephen said that after Manuel had worked for him, he had hired "a Frenchman" for a period. Somehow, the police ignored investigating that farmhand, although Manchester said he had left town after quitting the farm.

To their credit, the police did a good job of establishing that "Manuel" was actually Jose Correiro (de Mello). And, at least according to later reports in the newspapers, they had established that Jose had purchased a pair of shoes before leaving Fall River. But there is no evidence they had anything else against him. However, they vigorously pursued him. They threatened Jacintho Muniz Machado if he did not quickly find de Mello and then immediately bring him in. He was sent under the pretense that the authorities wanted to ask de Mello what he knew about someone stealing a horse.

Once Machado produced de Mello, the police began intensive questioning. They noticed a small smear of blood on de Mello's shirt. De Mello said he had cut his head and apparently touched his wound and then his shirt. But this was days after the murder and there was no way of knowing if the shirt de Mello was wearing when he came into the station was the same one he wore on the day of the murder. (No type of blood test was available in 1893; in fact, blood stains could not yet be definitively identified as coming from a human.)

Arrest

Lizzie Borden

Lizzie Borden had testified on each of the three days of the inquest. Late on the last day, she was held in the courtroom area while the last witness, Fred Hart, testified that he could identify her as the woman who came into Smith's drugstore and attempted to purchase prussic acid, a powerful poison. At the end of Hart's testimony, Lizzie was taken to the matron's room. The arrest warrant issued on the previous Monday had never been served. Now a new warrant was drawn up. Once it was completed, Mayor Coughlin and Marshal Hilliard called Andrew Jennings at his home and told him Lizzie was about to be arrested. The warrant was not read, or an arrest made, until Jennings arrived. After Jennings waived the reading of the warrant, Lizzie was arrested.

Unlike other female prisoners, Lizzie was afforded the relative luxury of the matron's room. She was allowed visitors, who also brought food for her. The next morning, she was arraigned and immediately transported to the Taunton jail. By coincidence, the matron of the women's ward was the mother of an old classmate of Lizzie's.

Jose de Mello

Jose de Mello, as described, was heavily interrogated upon his arrival at the police station. He was arrested early the following morning, a Sunday. On Monday morning, he was arraigned and, like Lizzie before him, immediately transported to the Taunton jail.

Between Being Jailed and the Preliminary Hearing

Lizzie Borden

Lizzie was sent to Taunton on Friday, August 12. The preliminary hearing was scheduled to begin only ten days later, on Monday, August 22. Lizzie was transported back to Fall River for this hearing, but upon its beginning, the hearing was immediately continued until the following Thursday. It was felt that transporting Lizzie back to Taunton and then again to Fall River for only three days was not worth the effort, so for those days she was kept in Fall River. But, again, she was afforded special treatment, once more being kept in the matron's room from Monday through Thursday morning.

The preliminary hearing was unusually lengthy, lasting through September 1. Each night, Lizzie again was taken to the matron's room. And, again, she was allowed visitors of her choice.

Lizzie was found "probably guilty" and taken back to Taunton. Much wrangling occurred regarding the scheduling of her trial. It finally commenced on Monday, June 5, 1893. She was kept in Taunton for these nine months. There were complaints from some that she received special treatment during this time. The sheriff, Andrew Wright, denied this, although it must be noted he was the husband of the matron, the mother of one of Lizzie's childhood friends. Lizzie was known to order meals from local restaurants, but Wright said any prisoner was so allowed.

JOSE DE MELLO

Jose de Mello did not have the wherewithal to employ an attorney. Portuguese Consul da Costa hired Boston lawyer P. Henry Hutchinson to represent de Mello. Hutchinson claimed a minor illness and, at the last minute, Fall River lawyer Marcus Swift acted as lead counsel for de Mello. The preliminary hearing was held on June 22, 1893. Swift provided no defense, other than cross-examining Stephen Manchester. After that, Swift threw in the towel and de Mello was adjudged probably guilty and returned to Taunton.

Swift was able to buy time for de Mello by filing a plea of misnomer. However, the Portuguese support for de Mello quickly waned, at least as to contributions, and de Mello was thus once again without counsel. Given the lack of funds and the apparent hopelessness of the case, seemingly no lawyer wanted any part of defending de Mello at trial. When a trial date in January of 1894 was about to be set, the Court assigned the firm of Swift & Grime to represent de Mello. (Not surprisingly, there is no record of de Mello ordering in restaurant meals during his six months in Taunton.) Within two days, de Mello pleaded guilty to second degree murder, so no trial ensued.

The differences in treatment in the two cases were not limited to Jose de Mello. Consider also the treatment of the occupants of the respective residences.

That both the Borden and Manchester houses were murder scenes was quickly clear to the police. In the case of the Borden house, when the police arrived, present were Lizzie Borden, Bridget Sullivan, Alice Russell, Mrs. Churchill, Dr. Bowen, and Charles Sawyer, a neighbor assigned to keeping out the curious. Within a few minutes, John Morse arrived. He was visiting the Bordens but had been away from the house when the murders were committed. None of these people were asked to leave the house during the police search. Mrs. Churchill, Charles Sawyer, and Dr. Bowen eventually left, but Lizzie, Bridget, and Morse were not asked to vacate the premises that night. In fact, Alice Russell was allowed to stay overnight, and visitors came to the house that evening with no apparent restriction imposed by the police.

The house was searched again two days later. No one had been asked to leave in the interim or during the search.

Since Lizzie Borden was allowed to stay in her house, we therefore have the police leaving a person suspected of murders at the crime scene for several days. Any possible evidence is thus subject to being destroyed or hidden, so long as Lizzie could conceal her actions from the inhabitants of the house. During this period, Lizzie does something that might be suspicious in the cellar and burns a dress in the kitchen stove. While neither act can unassailably implicate her in the murders, certainly it is arguable either or both might have.

Compare this with the actions of the police at the Manchester house. Stephen Manchester had reported the murder of his daughter to the police. They soon discounted him, his son Freddie, and farmhand John Tonsall as suspects. After the police search, Dr. Dolan allowed reporters access to the house for half an hour.

Once the police were through that evening, the Manchesters and Tonsall were not allowed to stay in the house, even though none were suspects. Stephen Manchester was operating a dairy farm and thus was not able to move to a different location even if he was otherwise willing to do so. The three were forced to sleep in the barn. The police would not even allow anyone in to cook or heat water to clean the milk cans.

Manchester hired a lawyer to help him get back into the house, but the order was not lifted until June 2, three days after the murder.

We see that both Chaves and the newspapers were correct. The two suspects, as well as their families, were treated differently and, in fact, this occurred throughout the legal process. But, upon closer inspection, we see that it is even deeper than that, because the two situations were different.

Stephen Manchester ceased to be a suspect within a few minutes. Conversely, Lizzie Borden *started* to be a suspect within a few minutes. Yet, she was given free access to her house until the moment of her arrest, one week after the murders. Stephen was not allowed to occupy his house until three days after his daughter was killed.

Lizzie was kept at arm's length by the police for the five days before she testified at the inquest. Yet, other than her own testimony, it appears nothing new of substance was learned at the inquest that the authorities did not already know. Upon turning himself into police voluntarily, Jose de Mello was grilled mercilessly and without counsel.

Upon incarceration, Lizzie was given special accommodations and visitors had access to her. Even if Captain Harrington's version above is correct, de Mello had no such privileges. His visitors had to be involved in the case while Lizzie's did not.

The differences in their respective treatments are a combination of class and gender. Lizzie Borden had both on her side. She was on the verge of being upper class, at least as far as family wealth was concerned. She lived in a time when society saw the roles of men and women quite differently. Women were seen by men as unequal and, since men were the ones in power, women suffered in having limited and low-paying job opportunities. In 1892 Fall River, every city alderman, common council member, and city officer was male. So was every judge.

However, in Lizzie Borden's favor, men typically did not see women as capable of violent crime. In his closing argument at trial, prosecutor Hosea Knowlton told the jury:

> You will be slower to believe that it was in the capacity of a woman to have done it, and I should not count you men if you did not, but it was done (*Trial*, 1657).

Perhaps a female of the lower classes might be thought capable of violent crime, but Lizzie Borden was not one of these. It might be supposed that a higher-class woman was not beyond poisoning someone, but she would hardly be thought to be felling victims with a hatchet. Since juries were also all male, their probable assumption of this worked to Lizzie's benefit.

Jose de Mello was at the other end of the spectrum. A person of his gender would be assumed to have committed the crime. Beyond that, being Portuguese, he was in a subset of the population that was immediately suspect when a violent crime was committed. The police had to overcome a self-imposed threshold to consider Lizzie Borden to be a suspect. After that, many of the general public would impose a second threshold to consider her to be guilty. Being male and Portuguese, the thresholds imposed on Jose de Mello were in the opposite direction.

Also, the police had more to lose in the Borden case. Many wealthy citizens, plus two of the daily newspapers, immediately criticized the police for arresting Lizzie Borden. Out-of-town newspapers tended to agree. Ironically, the police were criticized for treating her too harshly. Had Lizzie later been shown to be innocent, or even, as it turned out, found not guilty, the state would have hell to pay. While Jose de Mello was, at least initially, supported with great vigor by the Portuguese community, that ethnic group had little clout in Fall River, and their dissatisfaction with the treatment of their countryman was probably not even considered by the police.

The criticism of the police in the de Mello case was, at least in print, limited to a few letters from the Portuguese community, and much of this was in response to his treatment after being arrested as opposed to outrage at his arrest. By comparison, everyone up to Massachusetts

Attorney General Albert Enoch Pillsbury was looking for cover in the Borden case.

Today, the accused must be told his or her rights upon being arrested and counsel is available immediately to all, even to those who cannot afford their own attorney. If these laws had been in effect in the 1890s, they might have affected Lizzie Borden somewhat, but there is no doubt they would have been in Jose de Mello's favor versus what he faced in 1893. However, in looking at much more recent cases of similar circumstances, one must wonder if things have really changed much. The rich woman accused of murder would be able to afford a top-notch attorney. The young Portuguese immigrant would be assigned an overloaded public defender. Social media world would be afire with criticism of the arrest of the wealthy woman but support for the young immigrant would likely be sparse.

While not directly connected to the treatment of Jose de Mello, it is offered here that de Mello's downfall was entirely self-inflicted. It is true that, as a Portuguese who had recently worked at the Manchester farm, de Mello was quickly a suspect, but the police had no other reason to consider him so.

Jose de Mello was eventually done in by buying a pair of shoes with two unusual coins. The nature of these coins led police to determine they had been owned by Bertha Manchester. It seems likely that de Mello did not intend to attack Bertha Manchester when he entered her house. His Fall River lifelines had run out and he was desperate for funds. He worked for Stephen Manchester a few times and thought there was money kept in the house, or perhaps had seen some valuables there.

Under this assumption, de Mello could arguably have never been connected to the crime had he not spent the two coins (and continued to avoid the temptation to fetch the hidden watch and sell it). All de Mello had to do was leave any items he had stolen (or was about to steal) at the Manchester house after killing Bertha. Fingerprinting was not yet conducted in the United States, so there was no way to trace anything handled in the house to him.

There is no doubt the police, for lack of a better suspect, would still have pursued de Mello. Let us assume they did have Machado bring in de Mello, as actually happened. They would have questioned him with equal vigor. But other than a small amount of untestable blood found on his shirt, now several days after the murders, absolutely no evidence would have connected to de Mello. This would be true in perpetuity unless de Mello slipped up and said something to somebody. But even then, he might be in the clear. De Mello did not speak English. He had no affinity to American culture and no connection with anyone other than his resident countrymen. But the Portuguese tended to have more loyalty within the group than with the rest of the community. Thus, even a slip by de Mello to a countryman might not have been reported to anyone outside that community.

Of course, had de Mello had the foresight to realize all this, he still would have been destitute after leaving the Manchester house. But we saw he did get employment in Taunton just a few days after the murders. In the end, a new pair of shoes cost him a life sentence in prison.

CHAPTER 12
AFTERWARDS

1894

Reward Money

Jacintho Muniz Machado (aka Jacinto Muniz), applied for the $500 reward authorized by the Fall River aldermen for information or actions resulting in the apprehension of the murderer of Bertha Manchester. Machado did not receive the award because Mayor Coughlin had never signed the authorization, even though it was he who requested it.

While this should have ended the matter, it did not. In February, shoe store owner Joseph Lacroix said he would put in a claim for the reward. According to the *Fall River Daily Evening News*:

> He submits that he furnished the principal witness (the Portuguese across the river,) and also nailed De Mello's connection with the case by *marking* [newspaper's emphasis] that Mexican dollar which the murderer gave him in payment for the shoes. (Feb. 23, 1894)

One would think the *Evening News* drafted this article based on speaking with Lacroix. However, his description makes no sense. Jose de Mello had offered in payment an intact trade dollar and a plugged fifty-cent piece. Even assuming Lacroix meant "trade dollar," or the newspaper misquoted him, there was never any mention of his marking it. Since Lacroix accepted the trade dollar, marking it made no sense. Even if he did so for some reason, a jury would have to believe Lacroix's story that this was the coin given to him by de Mello. What helped "nail" the case was Stephen Manchester's testimony that this coin was identical to one he once gave to Bertha and the confirmation of this by Jennie Coolidge.

On March 7, the *Daily News* reported that Machado's widow had also put in a claim for the reward on the grounds that her late husband caused the arrest of Jose de Mello.

On March 10, Joseph Lacroix, on a petition made by the Fall River law firm of Jackson & Slade, made good on his promise and filed a formal claim for the reward.

Since Jacintho Muniz Machado had not received the reward, the *Daily Herald*, not surprisingly, questioned whether either of the two new claimants would have any more success:

> A question has arisen as to steps which will be necessary for these parties to take to get possession of the reward. The first thing, after having filed their claims, will be to prove who has the best right to the money. When this is definitively decided according to the order of the board of aldermen passed last year the mayor is authorized to give an order upon the city treasurer for the amount of the reward, as stated in the order, from the contingent account.
>
> It is also probable that a question may arise as to the power of the mayor to make such a move under a board of government which has ceased to exist. It may involve a much mooted subject, and developments are awaited with interest. (March 10, 1894)

Although we don't know why it took so long to adjudicate the matter, on October 8, the city turned down Joseph Lacroix's claim to the reward. As one might expect, the reason, once again, was that the mayor never signed the authorization. The explanation for the refusal was submitted by Marshal Hilliard and City Solicitor George Grime. (Yes, the same George Grime whose firm defended Jose de Mello.) Told of the city's decision, Lacroix asked the aldermen to reconsider, since it was based on a technicality. They refused to do so, saying that they were satisfied that Hilliard and Grime had canvassed the case thoroughly.

The result of Mrs. Machado's claim does not appear in the newspapers, but her claim obviously would have suffered the same fate.

The Manchester Divorce

For some time, Mary Jane Manchester had attempted, with some success, at having Stephen pay separate support. This quest did not end upon the dismissal of the divorce actions:

> In the probate court today, before Judge Fuller, the case of Mrs. Mary J. Manchester, ptr., vs. Stephen C. Manchester, for separate support and maintenance, and custody of minor child was heard. T. R. Vestal and F. J. McLane gave expert opinion as to the value of certain land on So. Main street in which the respondent had an undivided interest. Mrs. Manchester rehearsed

the old story, and Judge Fuller interrupted. He saw that Judge Hopkins' decree, dismissing the libel of respondent, settled the fact that Mrs. Manchester lived apart for justifiable cause.

Judge Fuller decided that Mr. Manchester should pay $4 a week to his wife; that she should have the custody of the minor child, Alexander, 9 years old, and that respondent should pay $30 for this process. Milton Reed for the petitioner: A.J. Jennings for respondent. (*FRDG*, April 11, 1894)

It is difficult to assess why Lizzie Borden's lawyer, Andrew J. Jennings, had replaced A.E. Bragg as Stephen's attorney. In any event, Stephen's change of representation did not help. The temporary $3 per week payment previously decreed by Judge Blodgett was not permanently raised to $4 per week.

Trouble seemed to find Stephen in his older age. In November of 1894, while Stephen was in his barn, someone climbed through a window of his house and stole a gun.

1895

STEPHEN MANCHESTER ACCOSTED

In January of 1895, Stephen Manchester was in court once again, having brought charges against Daniel Murphy for assault:

Manchester - I was on Anawan street delivering milk when Murphy came up, called me a vile name and wanted 14 cents which he claimed that I owed him. Said if he didn't get it he would knock my head off. I told him to knock away and he threw a stone and struck me on the shoulder.

Murphy - I worked for Mr. Manchester and one morning he got mad, grabbed a pitchfork, and told me to get out. Then, because I spilled a little milk, he charged me 14 cents.

Manchester - Well, the truth about that matter is this. He got sassy and I discharged him. After that I gave him his breakfast and a ride to the city. In getting out of the wagon he tipped over two quarts of milk, and I made him pay for it. That's the reason he threw stones at me. I want to know if I can't have protection from such assaults.

Mrs. Murphy - I'm the lad's mother, judge, and all he had to eat at Manchester's was johnny cakes three times a day.

The Judge - Never mind that, he could have done worse. It's no excuse for throwing stones at this old man. He is fined $25. (*FRDG*, Jan. 14, 1895)

1897

STEPHEN MANCHESTER'S DEATH

Stephen Manchester did not marry until the age of thirty-five. His daughter Bertha was born in 1871, when Stephen was forty-two. At the time of Bertha's murder in 1893, Stephen Manchester, for the times, was an old man of sixty-four. By 1896, he was diagnosed with neck cancer and suffered two operations. Before a scheduled third operation could take place, Stephen had a heart attack and died on April 17, 1897. He was sixty-seven years old. Stephen had been in the newspapers a great deal in 1893 due to Bertha's murder and, in 1894, during his divorce hearings. Yet, when he died only three years later, he was a forgotten man. His death notice was only a few lines in the *Daily Evening News* and *Daily Herald*, saying he was "noted for his frugality and untiring industry."

One often hears the phrase that a particular action is causing someone to "turn over in his grave." If Stephen Manchester could have read the May 1, 1897, edition of the *Fall River Daily Evening News*, he might have entertained such an activity:

> Mrs. Stephen C. Manchester and her son are now living at the homestead on New Boston Road, with Mr. Manchester's son Frederick.

Stephen's failure to obtain the divorce he sought in 1893 meant that Mary Jane was still his wife, and thus entitled to share in his estate. (Of course, Alexander would as well.) His hated second wife now not only inhabited his home of three decades, but also, at least temporarily, oversaw the youngest child from his first marriage, who had no blood relationship with Mary Jane.

On May 7, Mary Jane was appointed guardian of Alexander, and Stephen's daughter Jennie Coolidge became the guardian of Freddie. She also became the executor of Stephen's estate, the value of which was listed as $300 of personal property and $3,000 of real estate. However, it would have to be assumed that this was an estimate for, on September 10, the *Fall River Daily Evening News* reported an inventory of the estate had been made. The numbers were now revised to $1,075 of personal property and $19,820 in real estate. This was a small fraction of Andrew Borden's wealth at the time of his death, but far more than the typical Fall River worker would leave to his heirs. Since Mary Jane was still his legal wife, it would be assumed she got a significant fraction of the estate.

Mary Jane died of "softening of the brain" on June 8, 1899. She was only fifty years old. In 1900, the U.S. census shows Freddie, now seventeen, living with three of Stephen's sisters, Mary, Lucannah, and Nancy Downing. Mary and Lucannah had never married; Nancy had been a widow since 1888. Freddie was employed as a teamster. He certainly had a difficult childhood. His mother died almost immediately after his birth. His stepmother was absent from the household for most of his childhood, and things were not peaceful there when she was present. He was the one who first found Bertha's body after her murder. His father died when Freddie was fifteen. He may have lived for a while, whether voluntarily or not, with the hated stepmother. Then, he lived with three elderly aunts. All this occurred before his eighteenth birthday.

Alexander Manchester was only fourteen when his mother died. A listing for him does not appear in the 1900 census, but later censuses show that he lived in Fall River the rest of his life.

1902 – 1906

ESTATES

Stephen's father, Benjamin, had acquired some valuable real estate by the time of his death in 1864. In 1902, Benjamin's property on South Main Street, between Spring and Rodman, went up for auction. The successful bidder was William Coolidge, the husband of Stephen's daughter, Jennie. He bid $16,500 for the property. Since the property was put up for sale by Benjamin's heirs, and Jennie was one of them, Coolidge would not have paid the full bid amount. The heirs also sold a triangular piece of land at Plymouth and Second Streets for $14,000.

In 1906, the estate of Stephen's brother Abraham was probated. Each of Stephen's surviving children—Harry, Jennie, Freddie, and Alexander—was awarded 1/32 of the estate. The appraisal of Abraham's property totaled $77,130. While this was a substantial sum in 1906, we see that the inheritance of each of Stephen's children was a much more modest $2,400.

CHAPTER 13
JOSE CORREA DE MELLO

Being in prison for the rest of one's life cannot be pleasant under any circumstances. But, if there is a curve to measure the level of unpleasantness, Jose de Mello was arguably near the bottom end of it.

First, he was only nineteen when he began his sentence. Prison life was difficult, both physically and psychologically. Perhaps he had only twenty years left to live. But, at his young age, he might have had fifty. And, it will be recalled, Judge Braley did not issue a sentence of life imprisonment, but life imprisonment at hard labor. Labor assigned to the prisoners included the making of shoes, chairs, wood moldings, quilted molding, harnesses, and hats.

The prison, itself, must be considered. Charlestown, Massachusetts, was laid out in 1829, a year before the town of Boston was founded. The prison was built in 1805 on Lynde's Point, about one-half mile south of the site of the Battle of Bunker Hill. Although now a peninsula, at the time, Charlestown was an island with only one bridge to the mainland. Thus, the prison's location was selected with security in mind. In its initial configuration, the prison had 90 cells, each 9 feet by 8 feet. An 1829 expansion added 304 cells; another in 1850 added 150 more, for a total of 644.

By May of 1878, the prison was considered obsolete. All the prisoners were moved to a new prison in Concord. But only six years later, in 1884, the state legislature decided the Concord facility was to be used for younger prisoners who could be rehabilitated. Rather than building a new prison for the displaced prisoners, the decision was made to renovate the old Charlestown facility. The term "renovate," however, should be considered loosely—mostly it involved cleaning out accumulated debris and whitewashing the walls. In the Concord facility, each cell had its own water closet. Prisoners returned to Charlestown again had only a sanitary bucket in each cell.

It was to this "renovated" prison that de Mello was sent to live out his years.

While the Portuguese community seemed resigned to believe de Mello had killed Bertha Manchester, they did not entirely abandon him. Consul da Costa visited de Mello in Charlestown from time to time. In June of 1895, da Costa visited Fall River. He told of his visits with de Mello. He said de Mello once again repeated his story of how the crime was committed. Jose de Mello told da Costa that he went to the Manchester house in the hopes of getting money he felt still owed to him by Stephen Manchester. Going in the house, he found it empty. He decided to steal two dollars he found on a bureau. While attempting to exit through the kitchen, Bertha came in from whatever chore she had been doing in the yard or barn. She said something to de Mello but, of course, he did not understand her. She then grabbed the axe from the wood box and lunged at him. He evaded the blow, and she attempted a second attack. In the process, she dropped the axe. De Mello was able to pick it up, but Bertha grabbed him by the throat. A struggle ensued in which he eventually overpowered her.

Consul da Costa told Fall River reporters that Charlestown officials considered de Mello to be a model prisoner.

Those researching their genealogy typically consult census records. The researcher may spend some time in these searches, often discovering an ancestor was not where previously thought in a given census. Sometimes, he or she cannot find the person at all. In the case of Jose de Mello, his whereabouts in 1900 were well known. While dry and matter-of-fact, the census can offer new information about a person. Such is the case with Jose de Mello.

In the 1900 census, the enumerator listed him as Jose Carrea de Mello. The inmates at Charleston are listed nominally in alphabetical order. This would lead one to believe that the census taker might have used prison records for his listings as opposed to interviewing each inmate personally, as it would be supposed that the housing of the inmates was alphabetically random. De Mello is listed as being born in February 1874. This indicates that de Mello was not long past his nineteenth birthday when he killed Bertha Manchester. He is shown to have been born simply on "Western Island." The Azores were also known as the Western Islands, especially by local inhabitants, but the casual researcher might not be aware of this. The only indication of his heritage is that his parents are listed as being Portuguese. The year of immigration is blank. De Mello is shown to be able to read and write English, but this is suspect, because every prisoner, save a few, is thus shown—this in a population rife with those who would be assumed to be uneducated and at a time when many civilians could not read or write English. De

Mello's occupation is recorded as "farm hand," which, in fact, was as close to an occupation as he had before the murders.

Jose de Mello may have been a model prisoner, but all was not well, at least as one might describe "well" under the circumstances. On October 13, 1900, de Mello was transferred from the Charlestown Prison to the state's mental institution in Bridgewater.

A later newspaper article gave some details:

CORREIRO VIOLENTLY MAD

> Manuel Jose Correiro and Jeremiah Manchester, committed to the State prison respectively for killing Bertha Manchester of this city and Alonso Tripp of Westport, are insane. Recently they were transferred [from] the State prison to Bridgewater State Farm on the possibility that the change might have a beneficial effect. There is a considerable insane department at the State farm run on similar lines to the regular State insane asylums. Attendance [sic] for the insane are in charge, who have no responsibilities in the other departments. (*FRDH*, March 21, 1901)

One is struck by the irony that the prisoner accompanying de Mello to Bridgewater was named Manchester.

The Bridgewater facility had been opened as an almshouse in 1854, but changed its purpose a few times over the years. In 1894, admissions were limited to insane prisoners and a division was formed the following year called the State Asylum for Insane Criminals.

In 1906, twelve years after de Mello was first incarcerated in Charlestown prison, the Portuguese community of Fall River was still involved in his case:

> A number of Portuguese people in this city are interesting themselves in a petition for the pardon of Joseph Correiro, now serving a sentence of 20 years for manslaughter for killing Bertha Manchester in this city on Memorial day, in 1893. Correiro has served 13 years of his sentence. He had an aged mother and father living at St. Michaels, Azores Island, who are anxious to see their son again before they die and the petitioners for pardon are asking for his release with the understanding that he will leave the country and go back to the Azores. (*FRDG*, Nov. 22, 1906)

The reasoning behind the community's request is nebulous. Certainly, many inmates serving a life sentence (not twenty years, as the article states) eventually have aging parents, and said parents have undoubtedly wished their son or daughter would be released. The fact that de Mello was a foreigner and would leave the country upon release is also a weak reason to free a man convicted of brutally killing a young girl.

In 1909, the State Asylum for Insane Criminals was renamed Bridgewater State Hospital.

The 1910 census indicates de Mello was still at that facility. Unlike the 1900 census, inmates here were listed in random order, so it is possible that the census taker actually spoke to each inmate. The census taker listed the prisoner's name as "John C. DeMello," born in Portugal. Once again, although listed as an alien, de Mello's year of immigration is blank. Casting doubt on the information in the 1900 census, the census taker recorded that de Mello could neither read nor write English.

Thus, it would seem that the saga of Jose Correa de Mello had come to an end. He was sent to prison for life in 1894, not yet having reached his twentieth birthday. He was in the state prison in 1900, as his sentence so dictated. In 1901, he had been transferred to the state insane asylum. In 1906, a small newspaper article indicated the Portuguese community was trying to have him freed, but their justification for doing so was vague, especially given the violence of his crime, not to mention he was supposedly insane. In the 1910 census, he was still in the asylum.

Yet the saga was not over. Although not publicized, the Portuguese community had continued its quest for de Mello's freedom. In its May 27, 1913, issue, the *Fall River Daily Globe* reported:

> Ten petitions in circulation in this city, New Bedford and Provincetown will be presented to the executive council Wednesday, June 9, when the formal application will be filed seeking a pardon for Jose Correiro de Mello, the slayer of Bertha Manchester. The murderer, who is serving a life sentence at the Charlestown prison, and relatives interested Frank Wager of 178 Columbia street, this city, and he has general supervision of the petitions.

On June 4, a delegation visited the Governor to ask for a pardon for de Mello. According to the *Fall River Daily Evening News*, the group comprised "Frank M. Silvia, F. Wager, Dr. H.A. Rosa and Representatives Harrington and Sullivan." According to the group, there were "extenuating circumstances," but the newspaper did not state what they were. The group assured the governor that de Mello would immediately leave the country if freed.

As to how things got to this point, we must again return to the determined coalescence of the Portuguese community of Fall River.

The Portuguese had been in New England since the sixteenth century. In the mid-1800s, sailors from the Azores (the Western Islands), a possession of Portugal, began emigrating to New England to join whaling crews. The immigration continued even as whaling declined, with the new arrivals working in the burgeoning textile mills and taking other menial jobs. It is this group that those in Fall River referred to as "the Portuguese." Jose de Mello had recently come from St. Michael (São Miguel) Island in the Azores.

Because it consisted of so many poor and uneducated workers, this was the ethnic group looked at first when an apparently random crime was committed. In fact, when the first policemen arrived on the scene after the murders of Andrew and Abby Borden a year earlier, they asked Lizzie Borden if her father had any Portuguese working for him at the family's farm in Swansea.

As with any group, some rose to the top. Many such New England citizens of Azorean descent acted as leaders, attempting to steer their countrymen through the seas of American life. Although not part of any larger official group, the Portuguese from the various New England communities were known for sticking together when a countryman needed help or faced accusations.

As soon as Jose de Mello was arrested, help arrived immediately, from as far away as Boston. Let us first look at those who rallied behind him in 1893.

Fall River

Frank M. Silvia was born on St. George Island in the Azores on March 2, 1850. His family emigrated to the U.S., landing in New Bedford on August 15, 1866. He married another Azorean immigrant, Mary Doutra, in Fall River on August 30, 1874. In January 1881, the couple had a son, Frank M. Jr. Of him, we will hear more later.

Silvia had a sense for business and became a "licensed victualer," or, more basically, wholesaler and retailer of alcoholic beverages. However, he wore two hats, as he was also a steamship transportation agent.

Silvia founded the St. Joseph's P. B. & B. Society in Fall River, a benevolent organization for the Portuguese.

On the afternoon of June 3, 1893, Silvia told the police that he had heard Correiro was in Taunton. When Correiro was brought into the station that evening by his uncle, Jacintho Muniz Machado, Silvia accompanied the pair to act as interpreter.

Dr. Emanuel Dutra also emigrated from the Azores, as a young child with his father and mother. He was one of the attending physicians at the partial autopsies done of Andrew and Abby Borden on the afternoon of their murders. Of course, the Borden case had nothing at all to do with the Portuguese community, so it would be deduced that Dr. Dutra was a respected physician within the general population. He acted as an interpreter when Correiro was arraigned on June 5.

25. Frank M. Silvia Sr. From the *Fall River Daily Globe*, May 6, 1907.

Frank Peter (sometimes Peters) was born in the Azores about 1848. He married Ellen Brazile, also an Azorean, in 1887 in Fall River. At the time of the Manchester murders, he owned a grocery store at 8 Eagle Street. He claimed Jose Correiro boarded with him the night before the Manchester murders. On June 1, two days after the murder, he accompanied Inspector Martin Feeney to Tiverton, Rhode Island, following up on a tip that Correiro was there.

Jacintho Muniz Machado (also known as Jacinto Muniz) was the uncle of Jose Correiro. He was not a member of the Portuguese influential class and did not even speak English. After Silvia apprised the police that Correiro was likely in Taunton, they sent Muniz to bring him back to Fall River. Muniz did so the same evening. He was later ostracized by many members of the Portuguese community for bringing in Correiro, although it should be noted that police demanded he do so.

Manuel Sousa happened to be in the store of Joseph Lacroix when Jose Correiro purchased a pair of shoes there on May 30. Sousa was a laborer, not an influential member of the Portuguese community. He did not live in Fall River but rather across the Taunton River in Somerset.

After Correiro's arraignment, Sousa was kept on $2,000 bail as a material witness. The other material witness, store owner Joseph Lacroix, was not kept on bail. The difference appears to be that Lacroix was established in Fall River, whereas Sousa was young, probably poor, and lived in Somerset. It might further be speculated that police felt a fellow Portuguese might change his mind about testifying. Sousa's brother bailed him out.

Joseph M. Chaves was born on St. Michael in the Azores on February 3, 1865. Chaves immigrated to the United States on September 4, 1884, and settled in Fall River. He was first employed at the American Print Works. Eventually, he became a clothing clerk at Talbot & Co. and then C. E. Macomber Co. His background afforded his employer the ability to service members of the Portuguese community.

He quickly became fluent in English after arriving in Fall River and became an influential member of the Portuguese community, often acting as an interpreter at the district court.

In 1891, he was elected corporate secretary of the St. Joseph's Portuguese Society and president in 1893.

It was Chaves who first brought up the issue of what he considered unfair treatment of Jose Correiro by the police, by the sending of a letter to the *Fall River Daily Herald*, which they printed on June 13. With Vice Consul da Costa, Chaves visited Jose Correiro in his jail cell on June 14.

On March 30, 1894, a lost ten-year-old Portuguese girl showed up at the central police station. Police Matron Russell and others tried to communicate with her, but to no avail. Realizing they had to find someone to act as an interpretor, they called for Chaves, who was able to find where the girl lived and reunite her with her family.

As becomes true within any community, things were not always amicable. In the spring of 1895, Chaves applied to become a city constable. According to Chaves, Dr. Emanuel Dutra lobbied the board of aldermen to deny the application. It was only after Chaves successfully showed support by the Portuguese community as to his attaining this position that his application was approved on June 19. However, the successful appointment did not assuage Chaves's wounds. Chaves sued Dr. Dutra for slander the same day. The papers were returnable to court in August.

26. Joseph M. Chaves. From the *Fall River Daily Herald*, June 4, 1894.

Chaves might seem like an American success story. But his personal life was not a happy one. He married Margaret Campbell in 1886, but she died in June 1891. He remarried the same year, to fellow Azorean, Maria DeCaradozo. In late June 1895, Maria gave birth to a girl, Lillie, but the baby was blind and fraught with other abnormalities. About two weeks later, on July 8, their one-year-old son Alfred died of cholera. Four days after that, on July 12, before the court case against Dutra could be heard, Joseph M. Chaves died of pericarditis. He was only a few months beyond his thirtieth birthday. Lillie died on July 17 of marasmus (severe malnutrition), leaving a mother whom newspapers described as an invalid.

Augustin Percot of St. Annes Church accompanied Consul da Costa and Frank Chaves when they visited Correiro on June 14.

Apparently, his work for the Portuguese community was recognized beyond Fall River. According to the July 20, 1894, edition of the *Fall River Daily Evening News,* "A knightly order was bestowed by the king of Portugal upon Rev. Augustin B. Percot, of the Dominican order, curate of St. Anne's parish, this city."

27. Viscount de Vale da Costa. From the *Boston Globe*, August 30, 1896.

Boston

As now, Boston was the de facto capital of New England, and the most influential Portuguese lived there.

Viscount de Valle da Costa (Manoel P. F. d'Almeida) was born in Flores in the Azores about 1850. He was educated there and on mainland Portugal. He became associate justice of Flores and was the leader of the Progressive Royalist party. In 1887, Portuguese King Luis I appointed da

Costa to be vice consul to Boston. He became consul about two years later. He served in Boston for twenty-five years, until Republicans replaced the royalists in Portugal.

New Bedford

Joseph I. da Terra was born in the Azores in 1856 and immigrated to the United States with his parents in 1869, settling in New Bedford.

He accompanied Consul da Costa to Fall River for the preliminary hearing on June 22 and again on July 19 for the plea hearing. He appeared at these sessions at the request of Consul da Costa, but there is no evidence he played an active part in the case.

Support from the Portuguese community notwithstanding, it would seem like de Mello's being sentenced to life in prison in 1894 would have ended any hope for him. And, if anything, matters became dimmer. Those with the most influence had been Chaves, Silvia, and da Costa. On July 15, 1895, just eighteen months after de Mello went to prison, Chaves died. It was a similar fate for the other prominent Fall River Portuguese involved with de Mello—Frank Silvia. About October 1, 1901, Silvia fell down a flight of stairs. He never recovered from the trauma, dying on October 6. In Boston, Viscount da Costa had never claimed any involvement beyond making sure de Mello was treated fairly by the court system. He did visit de Mello in prison, but there is no indication he did anything beyond that. Thus, by 1913, none of the influential Portuguese originally involved with the case were fighting for de Mello.

But now, twenty years hence, the Portuguese community had an entirely new generation of activists. Those of this group were not born in the Azores but showed no less zeal for their cause than did their Azorean-born parents before them.

Recall that Frank Silvia had a son, Frank M. Jr, in 1881. Now, in 1913, Frank Jr. was a lawyer. Like his father before him, Frank Jr. was active in Portuguese causes. Whether it was due to this general involvement or because he was trying to carry on some legacy of his father regarding de Mello, Silvia became involved in the de Mello situation.

A 1920 *Fall River Daily Globe* article reported of Silvia:

> He was admitted to the bar in 1911, and began practice in Fall River with offices in the Academy building and has made rapid progress. He has won special recognition as a trial lawyer and has won cases with the largest verdicts rendered in Bristol

county, the $7700 verdict in the Mediros case last April being one example. He demonstrated exceptional ability in the famous Retkovitz murder case and other important cases. (July 24, 1920)

But the purpose of the *Globe* article was to announce the nomination by the governor of Silvia as an Associate Justice of the Second District State Court in Fall River. He had also been chairman of the District One Draft Board during World War I.

The Retkovitz trial occurred in 1915 and the Mediros case in 1920. Therefore, all the above accomplishments took place after the 1913 petition. However, it seems likely that, by 1913, Silvia's expertise and zeal were already being recognized, even outside of the Fall River Portuguese community.

28. Frank M. Silvia Jr. From the *Fall River Daily Evening News*, May 18, 1914.

29. Frank Wager. From the *Fall River Daily Evening News*, April 28, 1913.

Frank Wager had a humbler background; he was a barber, with a shop at 275 Hope Street. Wager was born in Massachusetts on September 25, 1873. Although the name does not sound Portuguese, records indicate both of his parents were born in the Western Islands. In 1913, he was the secretary of the Portuguese Azorean Operative Beneficent. He was the Grand Marshal of the large parade held for the Portuguese celebration of the feast of Ecce Homo on April 28 of that year.

There were several Portuguese clubs in Fall River in 1913. **Dr. Henry A. Rosa** was prominent in the Portuguese Instructive and Naturalization Club. When a proposal was put together to form a council of representatives from each of the Portuguese clubs to better serve the Portuguese community, Rosa was named its first president.

30. Dr. Henry A. Rosa. From the *Fall River Daily Herald*, April 20, 1917.

As the names reveal, Harrington and Sullivan were not Portuguese. But Edward F. Harrington and Thomas D. Sullivan were the State Representatives for the Fall River area in the Massachusetts House. Both were Democrats, as was Governor Eugene Noble Foss.

On June 23, the *Daily Globe* reported that the petition would be presented to the Governor during that week. It added:

> For the past 20 years Mello has divided his time almost equally in a prison cell and the insane ward. The petition for his release has been in circulation now for some time. The last step, prior to the presentation of the petition to Gov. Foss, was taken at Charlestown prison yesterday by Frank Wager, who is associated with Frank M. Silvia of this city in the effort to free Mello. . . In looking up Mello's record as a prisoner and a patient in the insane ward, Mr. Silvia states today, the only mark against him during his 20 years of confinement was dated September, 1895, when he was placed in solitary confinement for four days, for cooking in his cell. (*FRDG*, June 23, 1913)

While slightly delayed, the petition was filed at the State House on July 2. It included an affidavit, signed by Jacintha Vieira Valozo, "stating that he would take care of de Mello for the rest of his life or he will send him back to his parents in San Miguel, Azores, if he prefers to go there" (*FRDG*, July 2, 1913). A letter was also included from the Bridgewater State Farm chaplain, Rev. Fr. James J. Murphy, in which he stated de Mello was one of the best prisoners ever confined in the facility. He heartily endorsed de Mello's release, saying this opinion was shared by the facility's physician, Dr. Barker. The signers of the petition were from all over the state:

> It is expected that Governor Foss will give his attention to the matter within a few days and decide whether or not he cares to refer it to the pardon committee of the executive council. The conversation which the Fall River legislators had with him several weeks ago, however, convinces them that he will take this action, and the committee will then decide upon a date for hearing the matter. (*FRDG*, July 2, 1913)

A July 15 article in the *Fall River Daily Herald* reported that the matter was closed, however:

> Gov. Foss today positively declined to send the petition for pardon of Jose Correira de Mello, murderer of Bertha Manchester, to the Executive council and directed that the matter be closed with the filing of all papers in the executive office. The Governor communicated his decision to Atty. Frank M. Silvia, who represented the petitioners, at a conference in the State House this noon. This action of the Governor means that de Mello must remain in prison until he dies, unless, of course, some governor in the future can be prevailed upon to pardon him. (July 15, 1913)

According to the *Daily Herald*, this decision was based at least in part on a report the governor received from J.H. Whitney, chief of the district police. Whitney had assigned Detective James J. Macksey to investigate the circumstances.

Macksey is quoted as follows:

> "Mrs. W. W. Coolidge of 278 Franklin street, Fall River, sister of Bertha Manchester; Frederick Manchester, 2674 North Main street, a brother; Lucy Manchester 285 South Main street, an aunt, and Mrs. Jessie Darling, also of 285 South Main street, a cousin, are all opposed to the petition for a pardon of Jose Correira de Mello."

Macksey said that Assistant Marshal William Medley (the same person who found no footprints in the Borden barn loft more than twenty years earlier) was also against the pardon. Medley said the crime was brutal and added, "that the reason the government accepted a plea of second degree murder was on account of the large expense incurred by the county in the Lizzie Borden murder case which preceded this murder and was under investigation at the time."

Macksey quoted Dr. Dolan's report that Bertha was struck twenty-one times with an axe. Further, de Mello did not surrender himself to police, but rather was decoyed to go to the station. Macksey also said that de Mello "has only been discharged from Bridgewater approximately three and one-half months as cured of insanity."

So, once again, the matter appeared to be settled. The Portuguese had made their case, but when Governor Foss investigated the matter, he seemed satisfied the state had acted properly in 1893.

But, on the day after the *Daily Herald* article, the *Fall River Daily Globe* had a different angle. In an interview, Frank M. Silvia told the newspaper:

> "Yes, I was at the State House yesterday and had a conference with His Excellency the Governor. The interview was short, but a very pleasant one. No, the governor did not turn down the petition, as was stated in the Herald last night. His Excellency thought that the present was not the best possible time to send the petition to the pardon committee. The governor's last words to me were to let the matter rest for the present, and take it up with him again in October. His reasons for doing so were made known to me." (July 16, 1913)

No information on the pardon issue appeared in the newspapers after the one in the *Fall River Daily Globe* on July 16. Then, out of nowhere, on December 31, all three Fall River dailies had page one stories on the de Mello pardon. Each was similar to the *Fall River Evening Herald* one quoted below:

> Frank M. Silvia, Esq., who, for the past three years has been acting as counsel for Mello in attempts to secure his release, accompanied by City Solicitor George Grime, appeared this morning before the executive board in behalf of the pardon. Frank Wager of this city, prominently identified with the movement, was also present.
>
> A previous attempt made this year to secure the pardon of Mello was opposed by relatives of the victim, by officials of the local police department and by various persons who have been acquainted with him during his imprisonment. Much testimony before the board in favor of Mello's release was given today and was of material value in bringing the matter to a conclusion. The agreement to deport Mello, while not entering in the original application for release, is in keeping with the plans of friends, who at the previous hearing expressed their intention of sending the prisoner back to his native town on St. Miguel Island, in the Azores group, where relatives reside. (Dec. 31, 1913)

This report confirms that Frank Silvia's statement to the *Fall River Daily Globe* on July 16 had been correct.

It was not until much later, in November of 1915, that a newspaper reported a detail of executive board hearing:

> Attorney Silvia, when the hearing was held, provided an unusual feature when he brought De Mello before the parole board and had him tell the story of his life and the circumstances attending the murder of the young woman. He was assisted at the hearing by City Solicitor George Grime of this city, who was counsel for the prisoner nearly 20 years before. (*FRDG*, Nov. 23, 1915)

On Thursday, January 29, 1914, the *Fall River Daily Globe* reported that Jose Correa de Mello would be released from prison the next day. The release was apparently timed in conjunction with a White Star ship sailing from Boston to the Azores on Saturday, January 31. It was said de Mello would return to live with his parents.

For some reason, the release did not take place according to this schedule, but rather on the morning of the ship's sailing. De Mello had to be hurried by friends down to the dock, where he boarded the *S.S. Canopic* for the Azores. The June 15, 1914, edition of the *Fall River Daily Globe* reported:

> Attorney F. M. Silvia has received a letter from Antonio [sic] C. Mello who was pardoned last January on the charge of the murder of Miss Bertha Manchester of this city, announcing that he has reached St. Michael's Azores Islands, safely. The condition on which the pardon was granted was that he at once leave this country and rejoin his parents in his native land. Attorney Silvia was one of those who interested themselves in circulating the petition for his pardon.

Let us review. A convicted felon is in jail. The two options presented are to have him serve out his term or release him. The victim's family wishes for the man to remain in prison. The assistant marshal recounts the violence of the murder, and the medical report indicates she was struck twenty-one times with an axe. The prisoner confessed to the crime and pleaded guilty. The judge applied the sentence as instructed by the law. Further, given all this, it would seem reasonable to assume that most citizens in Massachusetts would support de Mello serving out his sentence.

Those wanting to free de Mello comprise one relatively small population. Further, they are not claiming his innocence, albeit it was reported they proffered the weak argument that de Mello acted in self-defense. However, it would then have to be considered that said "self-defense" was because of his entering the Manchester house with thievery in mind. Bertha Manchester, finding de Mello there for illicit purposes, took the reasonable action of arming herself to drive him from the house. All right, might say his supporters, but he has aging parents he would like to see and would leave the country if freed.

Given these two options, the choice of what to do seems easy. But, notice that those wishing to keep de Mello in prison made their case through interviews with Detective Macksey. He, in turn, wrote a report for Chief Whitney. The chief then submitted the report to the Governor or his representatives. Those in the general population who wished de Mello to stay in prison were a silent majority.

By contrast, those supporting de Mello not only got multiple audiences with those in power, but they were also influential members of their community. If we are to believe the later newspaper article, de Mello himself was allowed to address the board. Jenny Coolidge, Freddie Manchester, and Assistant Marshal Medley had no such opportunities. Apparently, the personal pleadings of the Portuguese leaders and the two state representatives, along with the unnamed extenuating circumstances were sufficient to sway the governor and pardon committee absent any organized resistance.

One cannot help but see here yet another difference between the Borden and Manchester cases. Early on, Lizzie's friends and peers, along with much of the press, rushed to her defense. The local police handled her with kid gloves. However, after her trial, public palpable support for Lizzie waned. While she still had friends, she was seen by many as a novelty and gawked at in public. Not surprisingly, this caused her to become reclusive.

After the murder, Jose de Mello had no public support, save some from the Portuguese community. He was poor, a foreigner of the lower classes, and unfamiliar with the English language or the American legal system. The police treated him as such. He was sentenced to life in prison, with seemingly no hope. Yet, through diligent work by his countrymen, he eventually became a free man. He returned to his native country and certainly had a freer life from that point forward than did Lizzie Borden.

CHAPTER 14
AFTERTHOUGHTS

With Jose de Mello's 1914 letter to Frank M. Silvia, we have come to the end of the Manchester murder saga.

Let us consider the many facets of the case.

First, we have the mysterious murder of an innocent farm girl in Fall River, Massachusetts, in May of 1893. But was not some innocent girl killed in Chicago or New Orleans or San Francisco around that time? No books have been written about them; in fact, we do not even know their names. Yet two of the three daily Los Angeles newspapers ran the story of Bertha Manchester's murder on page one, and the third on page two. How could this be?

The answer lies in the murders of Andrew and Abby Borden in Fall River ten months earlier. That case has gripped the country ever since. As it happened, the trial of Lizzie Borden was to begin within a week of the killing of Bertha Manchester. Many in Fall River were incensed at their first whiff that Lizzie Borden was suspected. As each chapter of the case unfolded—the arrest of Lizzie after the inquest, the finding of "probably guilty" after the preliminary hearing, and the now coming of the trial—her supporters grew in ardor. Their consensus was that police too quickly concentrated on the "socialite," ignoring pursuit of other suspects. Andrew and Abby Borden were killed with a hatchet or a like weapon, and now, almost a year later, could that killer have murdered Bertha Manchester in a similar fashion? The *Los Angeles Times* article did not begin with the victim's name, but rather:

> [Fall River] is in a state of intense excitement tonight, due to the discovery of an atrocious murder, rivaling in many respects those of Mr. and Mrs. Borden (May 31, 1893)

We thus see that the Bertha Manchester case received some national attention only because of the Borden murders. There is no question that the *Los Angeles Times* would not have reported the Manchester murder had the Borden murder not happened. On June 5, the *Los Angeles Times* reported:

> José Carriere, suspected of the horrible murder of Bertha May Manchester, is under arrest in the central police station, charged with the crime. That he really committed the murder there appears to be little room to doubt in view of developments made in the investigation, which ended this morning. (June 5, 1893)

This two-sentence article is shaky. The suspect's name is misspelled but, more importantly, there was still some doubt as to de Mello's guilt at that point. But the newspaper seemed satisfied that this arrest somehow decoupled the Manchester and Borden cases. With that, they were done with the Manchester case. It was never again mentioned in that newspaper, but it continued to cover the Borden case through Lizzie's acquittal.

We have thus spent more than one hundred pages here describing a murder that, arguably, was no more newsworthy than other murders committed in the United States, even on the same day.

I came across the Manchester case during my research of the Borden murders. Its importance centered on the fact that Bertha Manchester was killed on May 30, 1893. Jose de Mello turned himself in on the evening of Saturday, June 3. The newspapers for that day were thus already distributed. The Fall River newspapers printed extras the next day as to the police having Correiro in custody. (The Sunday edition of the *Boston Globe* reported it also.) Jury selection for the Borden case began Monday, June 5. The selection was completed that day and the jurors were immediately sequestered for the remainder of the trial. They were not allowed to read newspapers.

Although the trial was in New Bedford, about fifteen miles from Fall River, the Manchester case had been publicized all over New England. Thus, as the theory went, those on the jury almost certainly knew of the Manchester case and that Bertha was killed with an axe. They might have heard that a suspect had been held by the police. If so, they would have known little of him, except that he did match the generic profile of those suspected of such crimes. Therefore, could not this person have also killed the Bordens? Although the Manchester murder was not mentioned at the Borden trial, might one or more of the jurors at least considered this possibility that Jose de Mello, not Lizzie Borden, wielded the hatchet that killed the Bordens?

A few of the jurors were interviewed after they rendered their not-guilty verdict for Lizzie Borden. None of them mentioned the Manchester case at all, although that does not definitively discount the possibility it was discussed during deliberations. However, the overriding point is that, with respect to those interested in the Borden case, the Manchester murder is mentioned only in connection to those crimes. If it can be shown that Jose de Mello did not kill the Bordens, which certainly is the case, interest in the Manchester case disappears.

But, in my research, the more I read about the Manchester case the more I realized it needed an afterlife of its own. In the Borden case, we have two people murdered with a hatchet. Bertha Manchester was killed with an axe. The two cases begin in essentially the same place. After that point, they could not have been more different. Yet, it became obvious to me that the Manchester case has every bit as much intrigue as that of the Bordens.

The two cases reek of gender and class differences. Bertha Manchester was killed in a manner equally gruesome as that employed on the Bordens. The axe blows to Bertha's head were just about the same in number as the hatchet blows to Abby Borden's head. Depending on one's position on the matter, if one supports Lizzie Borden being the murderer, she might have attacked her father and stepmother based on some transgressions done (or imagined to have been done) against her. But no one has ever suggested Bertha Manchester was anything but a totally innocent farm girl. Therefore, on paper, the two crimes should have received similar coverage, Obviously, they did not.

Bertha's crime was "typical." Someone tried to rob her house. She attempted to fight off the intruder but was overpowered. The assailant was a man from a minority community. Nothing about the Borden murders was typical. A well-off man and wife were butchered in their middle-class home only one short block from the downtown business district. An intruder would be suspected, but early on this theory becomes tenuous. First, the house was religiously locked. Secondly, there were two other inhabitants, neither of whom saw or heard anything unusual. Thirdly, medical examinations indicate the victims died at least one hour apart, meaning even if an intruder was able to enter the house undetected, he had to remain so for an hour after committing the first murder. The daughter of the male victim tells the police and, later, the prosecutor what she knows, but her story is rife with inconsistencies, and she is subsequently arrested.

It makes sense that the Borden case, by its nature, would receive extended coverage, even outside of Fall River. But, in this book an important point is shown: Even the "typical" murders have backstories. Certainly, Bertha Manchester was no less dead than were the Bordens. Whether guilty or not, Lizzie Borden did not visibly demonstrate any sign of mourning. It might be added that her sister Emma, who certainly had no involvement in the crime, did not publicly display any more grief than did Lizzie. Of course, one must be careful with such assessments but, in comparison, Stephen Manchester was clearly distraught over his daughter's death. Bertha's estranged older brother, who had not spoken to the family in years, immediately came to Fall River upon learning of his sister's murder. Bertha's aunt protested to the police regarding the removal of Bertha's body to the funeral home, lest the body be desecrated in the manner of the Bordens. Stephen Manchester's son-in-law protested that Stephen was not being treated fairly by the police or the general public. The point, then, is that every murder has a profound effect on the survivors.

We also see that every murder has a background beyond the crime itself. Let us compare the Borden and Manchester cases in that regard.

Mainly because of his wealth, Andrew Borden's history has become well known. He came from relatively modest beginnings. He opens a furniture business with a partner. In 1863, his first wife dies. Left with two young girls, he remarries. He adds undertaking services to his portfolio. After operating these businesses for some time, he sells both and, for the last fifteen or so years of his life, grew his assets into a relative fortune through investments and land acquisitions. It can certainly be argued that this Horatio Alger story might hold interest for some. But, on these pages we have also seen the background of Stephen Manchester. From an even humbler beginning, Stephen turned to whaling at an early age. For those reading *Moby Dick*, published about the same time that Stephen was plying the seas, the book gives insight as to Manchester's experiences during those years. Apparently saving his money during his whaling years, Stephen leaves the profession and buys property on the northernmost fringes of Fall River. He develops this into a dairy farm and then delivers milk daily around the city. His first wife dies; his second marriage does not work out. His teenage daughter has to quit high school in order to run the house and help care for her young brother. By the time of his death, despite all the obstacles thrown at him, although hardly approaching the wealth of Andrew Borden, he is relatively well-off. Is this a less interesting story than that of Andrew Borden?

With respect to the victims, is Bertha Manchester somehow a less interesting study than Andrew and Abby Borden? We have seen Andrew's background. Abby Borden's background is nondescript. She was a thirty-seven-year-old spinster at the time of her marriage to Andrew. After the murders, some effort was made to discover her background, but none of any significance was unearthed. We do not know much about Bertha, but her character was front and center after her murder. Her older sister Jennie had graduated from high school. Bertha, too, had this expectation, but had to quit school to keep house, help care for her younger brother, and tend to farm work. She probably had good reason to complain about her fate, but no such complaints were evident. When others encouraged her to come downtown to enjoy Memorial Day festivities, she instead stayed home to do farm chores. She had no suitors. This may be by happenstance, but it may also be she had no time for them. She had such little time to spare that she could not even go to church most Sundays.

A general commonality in the two cases is that both Lizzie Borden and Jose de Mello had supporters. In Lizzie's case, many of the wealthy and most newspapers thought her to be innocent. Women of all classes flocked to her defense. The prosecution found itself fighting these foes as much as the defense counsel. At least as far as visibility is concerned, however, these groups lost interest in her once she was found not guilty. Lizzie spent the rest of her life, to some extent, a social recluse because of all the interest she attracted when she went about town. But there were no newspaper articles or social groups demanding she be allowed a "normal" life.

In comparison, Jose de Mello had the support of much of the close-knit Portuguese community of New England even before he was arrested. This did not wane during his incarceration, with the exception that donations for his legal expenses dried up. But, as we have seen, the Portuguese did not give up on de Mello even after he pleaded guilty to murder. He was sentenced in 1894, but a 1906 newspaper article stated there were those seeking his release from prison. In 1913, twenty years after the murder, a group of Portuguese was able to convince the Commonwealth to free de Mello, after which he returned to his homeland. Is not the support for de Mello just as interesting as that shown for Lizzie Borden? In fact, is it not more so?

We see that on many levels, the essentially unknown case of the murder of Bertha Manchester is as interesting as the murders of Andrew and Abby Borden. But Bertha Manchester, and her killer, were of the lower social classes. It was seen as just another murder of a nondescript man or woman by a poor assailant of a minority class. One wonders how many other Bertha Manchesters existed about whom we know nothing.

ADDENDUM

1. Reconstructed Preliminary Hearing

The preliminary hearing in the Manchester case was held on Thursday, June 22, 1893, in Fall River. The three Fall River dailies and the *Boston Globe* all printed versions of the testimonies given at the hearing. None of the newspapers provided a stenographer, so their reporters took down the testimonies as best they could in longhand. Since they could not keep up with the spoken words, the reporters often took shortcuts and omitted parts that they either thought not critical or that they missed while writing something else. Given this, the four newspapers did not agree completely as to what was said, although the gist of each matched with the other three. The following, as best as can be done, combines the reports from the three newspapers.

After the witness had been sworn, the father of the murdered girl was called to the stand.

(No district attorney was present. The prosecution questions at the hearing were asked by Judge McDonough.)

Stephen C. Manchester

(Judge McDonough) Q. What is your name?
A. Stephen C. Manchester

Q. Where do you live.
A. On the New Boston road.

Q. How long have you lived there?
A. Twenty-six years.

Q. Did you live there on May 30 of this year, the day Bertha died?
A. Yes.

Q. Did you leave home that day?
A. Yes.

Q. About what time?
A. 7:30 in the morning.

Q. When was the last time you saw Bertha alive?
A. When I left on my milk route Bertha was on the doorsteps all alone.

Q. What time did you return home?
A. Between 2:30 and 2:45 in the afternoon.

Q. What happened then?
A. On arrival, my boy Freddie jumped off the wagon and ran into the house to get something to eat. I went towards the barn. Just as I got inside Freddie came running out and told me that Bertha had been killed. I ran to the house and saw her lying on the floor with her legs bent up slightly and she was almost on her face. There was blood all around her. She was badly cut up and there were three dents in the back part of her head. She was cold and had been dead for some hours.

Q. Do you know anything, of your personal knowledge, how she came to her death?
A. No, sir.

Q. Did you ever notice that man? (*Obviously motioning towards Correiro.*)
A. Yes, he worked for me two days.

Q. How long before this murder?
A. Twelve or fifteen days.

Marshal Hilliard stepped forward and put a gold watch on the clerk's desk.

Q. Do you know anything about that watch?
A. Yes, that's Bertha's watch. I made her a present of it two or three years ago.

Q. Where did you buy it?
A. At Foster's, on Pleasant street.

Q. When you returned home did you search for the watch?
A. Yes, I went to her room and found the watch was gone.

Q. Did you miss anything else from Bertha's room?
A. Yes, her pocket-book.

Q. Could you identify it?
A. Yes.

Judge McDonough looked toward the marshal as if anticipating the production of the pocketbook, but the marshal shook his head. The pocketbook was not shown.

Cross-examination

(Mr. Swift) Q. Your business is farming and selling milk?
A. Yes, sir.

Q. How long have you been engaged in that business?
A. Twenty-five years.

Q. You say you have seen this person (*Correiro*) before; where did you see him before to-day?
A. He worked for me two days. The first time I saw him was along the first of November, or the last of October, 1892. At 5 o'clock in the afternoon he came up to the barn and said, 'Job for me?' I said, 'can you milk?' He said 'yes.' 'I'll try you then,' was my reply. I was cutting green barley then, and he went out and helped me. We afterward fed the cattle, did the chores, milked the cows, ate supper and went to bed. Next morning got up and did the chores. He ate breakfast and then left my farm about 6 o'clock. I didn't see him again till about the middle of May.

Q. Where did you see him?
A. I was milking in the barn and he came there with his coat on his arm. He wanted a job and I told him to take a pail and milk a cow. He sat down, milked some of the cows, got supper, went to bed and next morning I took him with me on the milk cart. We started away about 7 o'clock. We delivered the milk and went home about 1:30 o'clock. That afternoon we planted a bushel of potatoes.

Q. What did you do on the second day?
A. We delivered milk again and planted some more potatoes.

Q. What did you do on the third day?

A. He helped me to peddle milk till about 11 o'clock, and then he left me. We were about Charity Lane, on South Main street. He saw two Portuguese and went towards them. I went to deliver milk at Harry Howard's, and when I came back he was in conversation with those two men. One of the men came to me and asked what I was going to pay him (*Correiro*). I replied that he was a green hand and could not talk English. I would allow him $15 a month and board. I told him that he (*Correiro*) was a good milker. The Portuguese who was talking to me for him (*Correiro*) said that he would not stay for less than $20 a month and board. I replied that if I had to pay a "green" Portuguese $20 a month and board they could have him. I said, 'I shan't pay it.'

Q. Where was Correiro then?
A. On the sidewalk.

Q. What did you call him?
A. I called him 'Manuel.' I pointed when I wanted him to do anything.

Q. When again did you see him?
A. The second day after that. I was planting potatoes in the field. He had a little bag with him, such as Portuguese are often seen to carry their clothes in. I asked him if he had come to get his things, and he nodded. He got them. I gave him $1 for two days' work and he left seeming cheerful.

Q. About what time was that?"
A. About 3:30 or 4 o'clock in the afternoon.

Q. When he left which way did he go?
A. Down toward Wilson road.

Q. What did you call the Frenchman you had working for you?
A. I called him George; the other part of his name I did not know.

Q. When was the next time you saw Correiro?
A. On Pleasant street between Second and Third streets. He was leaning against a wagon. Freddie called my attention to him by saying: 'Why don't you hire Manuel? He wants to work for so much (*showing fingers*) a month.' I remarked: 'What's the use of hiring him? He comes one day and is gone the next.' Up near Scherer's store he got two Portuguese to talking for him. I told them he was a good milker and that I would pay $15 a month and his board. They both said: 'That is good for you.' He (*Correiro*)

consented to go home with me. He helped me do the chores that night; next morning he had breakfast and away he went again.

Q. When was the next time you saw him?
A. It was on the Crab Pond bridge on May 30, about 11 o'clock in the forenoon.

Q. How do you know it was 11 o'clock?
A. I looked at the Print Works clock immediately before and remarked to the boys on the team with me that we had just one hour to finish the route.

Q. Where was Correiro?
A. He was on the bridge heading north. I was going south.

Q. When was the next time you saw him?
A. Here at the station last Thursday.

Q. Had you any conversation with him on the bridge?
A. No; he turned his head and grinned.

Q. Where was the last place you left milk that morning?
A. At No. 35 Globe street.

Q. From there did you drive directly home?
A. No, I stopped at my sister's at 12:30 and then stopped at the corner of Borden street and bought $1.50 worth of flowers from Mr. Peckham of Little Compton, R.I. I was going to take them home to Bertha. I spent twenty minutes talking to Mr. Peckham and then went up Pleasant street to Oak Grove avenue and then home.

Q. Can you tell us more particularly about the time you reached the house?
A. I didn't look at the clock, but I think it was about 2:30. I drove very hard, but the day was warm, and I didn't get home before that hour.

Q. Didn't you get home before 1 o'clock?
A. No.

Q. Before 2 o'clock?
A. No. It is just four miles from my house to City Hall, no matter which way you go. I think I stopped at the grain store after I bought the flowers. Freddie and John were with me. John is not working for me now, he left the day I buried Bertha. When we got

home, Freddie jumped out, and went to the house to get something to eat. John opened the barn door for me, and I drove in. I put up my horse and fed him four quarts of oats. Don't believe I took the harness off. It took me two minutes to do this and then I ran into the house.

Q. How long does it generally take you to get home?
A. I have driven from the south end of Oak Grove avenue in about fifteen minutes. I can drive there quite easily in a half an hour. Some times it takes me two hours to drive from the City Hall home, the time depending on whether or not I meet anybody and what business I have to do on the way. The distance from my house to City Hall is four miles. I called at 'Joe' Cadieux's store at Stafford square that day to get some grain.

Q. Were the boys, Freddie Manchester and John Tonsall, with you during all that trip?
A. Yes, sir.

Q. How long has John worked for you?
A. He doesn't work for me now. He left the day I buried Bertha.

Q. How long did he work for you?
A. I don't remember.

Q. When you got home, who got out of the milk cart first?
A. Freddie. He went into the house to get something to eat. Then John got out and opened the barn door. I drove in. I put up my horse and fed him four quarts of oats. Don't believe I took the harness off. It took me two minutes to do this. Freddie called out that Bertha had been killed.

Q. As a result of what Freddie said after going into the house, what did you do or see?
A. I ran to the north door and stepped into the kitchen.

Q. Can you describe the layout of the kitchen?
A. There are four or five chairs and a stove in the room.

Q. What was the first thing you saw so far as Bertha was concerned?
A. She was lying on the floor, almost on her face, on the right side of the stove - a step and a half from the door. The distance between the door and the stove is about five-and-a-half feet. There was blood on the stove. The north door was shut and I opened it to get in. It is the nearest door to the barn. The other door on the south

side of the kitchen was open. These doors are completely parallel to each other by the compass. The south door is on the south side of the house. There is another door leading to the dining room.

Q. After you saw Bertha what did you do?
A. I went through the dining room and then to the sitting room north of it. All the doors were open except the kitchen door on the north side. In Bertha's room I noticed that things had been disturbed. A case on the top of the bureau had been opened and the watch was gone. In another room trunks had been opened and clothes were hanging out. I looked into the clothes press, and then went to my own sleeping room and saw that things had been turned over.

Q. Did you make an examination of Bertha?
A. I bent over and looked at her, but I never put a finger on her. God knows I couldn't.

Q. What position was she in?
A. She appeared to be trying to get up, poor girl.

Q. What wounds did you see?
A. There was one over the mouth and another on her forehead, but the biggest one was at the back of her head where the skull was broken in. I think there were three wounds on the back of the head.

Q. What did you do after discovering the murder and going through the rooms?
A. I quickly harnessed my horse and drove as fast as I could to tell the city marshal.

Q. Bertha was your housekeeper?
A. Yes, sir.

Q. How old was she?
A. About 22 years.

Q. How long is it since she left school?
A. About five years.

Q. She had attended high school?
A. Yes, but she didn't graduate.

Q. She had been doing house work for you six months prior to her death?
A. Yes, longer than that.

Q. How many cows did you keep?
A. Nineteen, and three horses.

Q. How big is your farm?
A. About 40 acres.

Q. How many barns have you?
A. Two, one is used for storage.

Q. How far is the barn most used from the door of the kitchen?
A. About 100 feet.

Q. Did you keep an axe in the house?
A. Yes. We use wood and coal in our stove. It is a large 'New Crown' one. The wood box stands back of the stove on the north side. The box is about 3-1/2 feet by 18 inches. The axe was kept in the wood box or along side of it, according to how full the box was. The axe was broken about two years ago. I broke it the first day I bought it, chopping the wood. I gave it to Bertha, telling her it was just the thing for her to chop kindling with. I don't know the condition of the wood box that day. The men generally kept it full. Bertha was burning wood that day. I saw the axe afterwards in the kitchen in the hands of a policeman. I do not know what time that was. I have not seen the axe since.

Q. Did Bertha usually split the kindlings?
A. She did sometimes.

Q. Have you seen the axe since?
A. Yes; covered with blood, in the hands of the police, in my kitchen.

Q. Who else was on the farm?
A. I had two boys and a Frenchman at work for me. The Frenchman had left off working for me. He worked until he earned $6.40, enough to take him away.

Q. What time did he stop working for you?
A. I don't know. If I had my book I could tell. It was about the 15th or 20th of May. I have not seen him since.

Q. What was Bertha's work?
A. She usually fed the horses, cattle and hens, besides the house work. They have the run of the farm in the daytime. At night they are kept in a hen house at the south of the barn. Bertha took care of them. They were generally fed on corn, scalded meal and

shorts. They had not been fed that day. Neither had the horses. Nothing had been done.

Q. What property did she have in her room on this morning?
A. I do not know just what Bertha had in her room. I had not been in there for three or four months. Last saw the watch about five months ago, when I took it to Foster's to be fixed. She had some rings and other trinkets, and a little boy's watch. She had a pocketbook - one to carry bills and a purse. I can't tell when I saw the pocketbook last. I have not seen it since the murder. I gave Bertha a trade dollar about 15 or 16 years ago. I do not remember the date. I didn't look at it. I had four of them at the time. I don't know when I last saw the trade dollar.

Q. Had she a half dollar with a hole in it?
A. Yes. I made the hole myself when she was a little girl. She used to have it on her wrist with a string through the hole when she was teething. She afterwards kept it as a souvenir. I don't know whether the hole was plugged or not. I cannot identify any of Bertha's money.

Q. Did she have any other jewelry in the room?
A. My little boy's watch and some rings.

Q. When did you last see these, before Decoration Day?
A. I don't know.

Q. Had she had them the last month?
A. I don't know.

Q. When the murder was discovered, what did you do?
A. Harnessed my horse and came to city hall.

Q. When you went to the city marshal's office, whom did you see?
A. I don't know the officer, I only stayed for a little while there.

Q. Where did you go then?
A. Then went to my sister's on Main Street. I stayed long enough to get her to go home with me.

Q. Did you go straight home from there?
A. I then called at Mrs. Coolidge's, got her, and drove directly home.

Q. What did you notice, when you got home?
A. Dr. Dolan and the officers.

Q. Had Bertha's body been moved?
A. No; it was in the same position.

Mr. Swift now examined the watch and then continued questioning Mr. Manchester.

Q. When did you get this watch?
A. I bought it at Foster's on Pleasant street, about two years ago last Christmas.

Q. Did you have it marked?
A. Yes; the case was marked B.M.M. The initials had been inscribed there by J.H. Franklin shortly after its purchase. (*The initials were found on the watch.*)

Q. Was Bertha in good health?
A. Yes.

Q. Did Bertha do any out-of-door work?
A. Yes; she ran the mowing machine, horse-raked and, in fact, did most any kind of work.

Q. Was she a strong, robust girl?
A. Yes; a very strong, industrious, hard-working girl. I was proud of her ability to do most anything. She was a good a child as God ever put a breath of life into.

Marshall Hilliard here presented a receipt given by Foster & Co. to Mr. Manchester at the time the watch was purchased. Its number is 2,377,280.

Q. What was the date on the coin - the trade dollar?
A. I cannot tell; don't know that I ever looked at the date.

Q. Did you know if she had spent it?
A. I am very sure she had not.

The witness then identified the receipts given for the watch and was allowed to step down at 11:10, after being on the stand a little more than an hour.

Mr. Manchester left the stand at 11:10.

F.M. Chase

Q. (Judge McDonough) What is your name?
A. F.M. Chase.

Q. What is your occupation?
A. I am a jeweler.

Q. Please look at this watch and tell me if you recognize it.
A. Yes. The serial number confirms I sold this watch to Stephen Manchester.

William A. Dolan

Q. (Judge McDonough) What is your name?
A. Dr. William A. Dolan

Q. You are the medical examiner for Bristol County?
A. Yes.

Q. Describe your actions on May 30 of this year.
A. At seven minutes past three in the afternoon, I received a telephone message saying there had been a murder committed at the Manchester place. Assistant Marshal Fleet and I drove there at once. We arrived there at 3:35 o'clock and drove around to the rear of the house.

Dr. Dolan was here interrupted, and defendant's counsel retired for consultation.

Court was given a recess of five minutes.

On returning, Lawyer Swift, speaking for the defendant, said he "thought it proper and suitable to waive further examination in this matter as far as the court is concerned."

The court then adjudged Correiro probably guilty and ordered that he be committed to the county jail without bail, to await the finding of the grand jury in the superior court to be held at Taunton next November.

2. Grand Jury Indictment of Jose Correiro

Commonwealth of Massachusetts.

Bristol SS.

At the superior court begun and holden at New Bedford within and for said county of Bristol, on the first Monday of June, in the year of our Lord one thousand eight hundred and ninety-three.

The jurors for the said commonwealth, on their oath and affirmation present that Jose Correiro of Fall River in the county of Bristol, on the thirtieth day of May in the year of our Lord eighteen hundred and ninety-three, in and upon one Bertha M. Manchester, feloniously, wilfully and of his malice aforethought did make an assault, and with a certain weapon, to wit: an axe, her, the said Bertha M. Manchester, feloniously, willfully, and of his malice aforethought did strike, cut, beat and bruise in and upon the head, face and neck of her, the said Bertha M. Manchester, giving to her, the said Bertha M. Manchester, by the said striking, cutting, beating and bruising in and upon the head, face and neck of her, the said Bertha M. Manchester, divers, to wit, twenty mortal wounds, of which said mortal wounds the said Bertha M. Manchester then and there died.

And so the jurors aforesaid, upon their oath and affirmation aforesaid, do say that the said Jose Correiro the said Bertha M. Manchester, in manner and from aforesaid, then and there feloniously, wilfully and of his malice aforethought did kill and murder, against the peace of the said commonwealth and contrary to the form of the statute in such case made and provided.

A true bill.

LUTHAN T. DAVIS, Foreman of the Grand Jury.

HOSEA M. KNOWLTON, District Attorney.

Bristol SS.:

On this thirtieth day of June, in the year eighteen hundred and ninety three, this indictment was returned and presented to said superior court by the grand jury, and ordered to be filed, and filed ; and it was further ordered by the court that notice be given to said Jose Correiro that said indictment will be entered forthwith upon the docket of the superior court in said county.

Attest: SIMEON BORDEN, Clerk.

A true copy. Attest: SIMEON BORDEN, Clerk

3. Plea of Misnomer

Commonwealth vs. Jose Correiro.

BRISTOL ss. SUPERIOR COURT,

July 19, 1893.

Now comes Jose Correa De Mello, who is indicted by the name of Jose Correiro, who in his own proper person pleads and says he was born in the village of Arrifes, in the island of St. Michaels, and that there after he was named, baptized and christened in his early infancy Jose Correa De Mello and by the name of Jose Correa De Mello has always, both before and since his baptism, hitherto been called or known: without this that he, said Jose Correa De Mello is not now and has not at any time hitherto been called or known by the name Jose Correiro, as by said indictment is supposed, and this he, the said Jose Correa De Mello is ready to verify; wherefore he prays judgment of the said indictment, and that the same may be quashed and abated.

my

JOSE CORREA (X) DE MELLO, Witness.

mark

Witness, JOSEPH I. DA TERRA.

Bristol, ss.

New Bedford,

July 19, 1893

Then and there personally appeared the aforesaid Jose Correa De Mello and subscribed the foregoing statement, and made oath that the statements therein contained are true, before me,

JOSEPH IGNATIUS DA TERRA,

Justice of the peace

BIBLIOGRAPHY

BOOKS
Martins, Michael and Dennis A. Binette. *Parallel Lives: A Social History of Lizzie A. Borden and Her Fall River*. Fall River: Fall River Historical Society, 2010.
Melville, Herman. *Moby Dick*. London: Arcturus Press, 2021. (Originally published as *Moby-Dick; or, The Whale*, 1851)
Spencer, William D. *The Case Against Lizzie Borden*. Knightdale, North Carolina: North Forest Press, 2020.

CENSUS RECORDS
Massachusetts State Census. Authorized by Massachusetts State Legislature, 1855 and 1865.
United States Census. United States Department of Commerce, 1820 to 1940.

DIRECTORIES
Boston City Directory. Boston: Sampson, Murdock and Company, 1893 to 1914.
Fall River City Directory. Various publishers, 1853 to 1930.
New Bedford and Fairhaven City Directory. Boston: W.A. Greenough & Co., 1893.

NEWSPAPERS
Boston Globe
Fall River Daily Globe
Fall River Daily Herald
Fall River Daily Evening News
Los Angeles Times

OTHER SOURCES
Widdows, Harry, Stefani Koorey, and Kat Koorey. *The Trial of Lizzie Borden: Three Volumes*. Fall River: PearTree Press, 2012.

WEBSITES
Ancestry
    https://ancestry.com/

Charlestown Historical Society.
    https://charlestownhistoricalsociety.org/chs_events/
        massachusetts-state-prison-charlestown/
New Bedford Whaling Museum
    https://whalingmuseum.org/
Social Network and Archival Content
    https://snaccooperative.org/ark:/99166/w6xtotsq
Unbottled
    https://unbottled.com/